FINDING YOUR

FREQUENCY

HOW TO BROADCAST
YOURSELF AND YOUR MESSAGE

JEFFREY A. SPENARD

Finding Your Frequency

©2016 Jeffrey A. Spenard

Perfect Publishing

ISBN: 978-1-942688-08-2

Printed in the United States of America

DEDICATION

I dedicate this book and give all the credit to my Father, God rest his soul, for making me the person I am today. My Dad and I are very alike in the fact that he was an outgoing, life of the party, help anyone with anything, give the shirt off his back kind of guy. I watched this from an early age not knowing at the time that I was inheriting his personality.

CONTENTS

PROLOGUE

Growing up in Smithfield, Rhode Island, a small town where everyone knows your name, it helped to make me the person I am today. Living in a great community and having a close family is where I learned the art of "one on one" conversation and building on your talents.

Not to toot my own horn, but when I was 9 years old, I was crowned "King of the Playgrounds", my Queen was Mayor Buddy Cianci's Daughter and that was out of 6 districts. When I was 11 I earned Boy Scout of the year and won a free trip to Camp Yago which at the time was $350 bucks!! Big money back then for my parents so they were as excited as I was.

When I was 16, not only was I working but, I was traveling Southern New England setting up rings and training to be a professional wrestler, the high flying, body slamming kind not the Olympic kind, which was going to be my career and my future.

As you can see I was never a shy kind of guy. Would I have ever thought then 30 years later I would be the CEO/Owner of World Talk Radio dba VoiceAmerica (www.voiceamerica. com) the pioneer of the world's leading live internet media broadcasting company I would have said you were crazy!

The fact that I am able to help box up and share your passions, dreams, talents and education with one other person or even a global audience gives me a strong sense of accomplishment.

Hopefully this book, and our continuing relationship and discussion will maybe make it easier for everyone to formulate, create and "get it out there".

I have paid the dues, fallen down a thousand times only to pick up and brush it off and traveled the roads not taken and now it's my pleasure to help you to learn from my mistakes and we can hopefully do it a better way.

Media can serve a purpose, but it needs to be engaging. We can't let it control us, we must control it. So do a show, don't do a show, but at least start a podcast, a Facebook Page, a Google Hangout, a LinkedIn group, or join VoiceAmerica, whatever it takes!

Take in the information from this book and on my website and make it your own. If you come up with a solid strategy, work with people that know what they're talking about, don't throw money around like you're a Rockefeller until you understand the basics, and have a commitment to a goal – you can pull it off like a rockstar!

Jeffrey A. Spenard

PS When you're done with this book, please feel free to call me, or email me with your idea for a show. www.jeffspenard.com

CHAPTER I
DEFINING
YOUR MESSAGE

The first step to creating a successful, long term talk radio or television show is defining your message.

It's important to understand that many different aspects of planning are intertwined and your end result will most likely change as you go through the steps and you combine your message, your audience, your goals and your strategy into a cohesive plan.

What do I mean by message?

Considering that your show will not be a "one off" enterprise, but will consist of at least several "episodes" at a minimum, but more likely be an ongoing success, your message starts by defining a "genre" or "theme" or "format."

If you are a connoisseur of talk radio you've probably already got a handle on the "format" of your ultimate show.

1

Depending upon which "platform" you select, and which provider you choose you might have a lot of expert help when putting together your show. For example, at VoiceAmerica you have a dedicated team working on all segments of getting your show ready to launch, whereas you might choose to go it on your own and essentially self-produce your show.

Either way, here are the basics that you need to know.

1. **Pick a theme or format for your show.** Before you even think about getting in front of a microphone you want to decide on an overall purpose for your show.

   It is quite possible to be successful with a "variety" show, however, in my experience over the past 20 years, you will be more successful if you have a "purpose" that you define before you get started.

   So before we talk about genres, let's talk about your purpose, which we will revisit under Chapters 2 and 4 coming up.

   Some hosts want to sell books, find clients, spread a message of hope, establish their credibility, try for a terrestrial radio syndication deal, generate traffic for a website, educate the populous on a new philosophy, make people laugh, promote the arts, espouse a political philosophy, or sometimes just always wanted to have a radio show.

You don't have to completely lock yourself into one of those "purposes", but you do need to ask yourself a few simple questions and ponder them for a moment or two.

- What is my show about?
- What would I like to listen to on my show?
- Is there a successful talk radio show that I would like to emulate?
- What can I do that's new?

Below are a few common talk radio show genres to get you started, but feel free to make up your own:

- News and current events

- Business and Financial --- this could be anything from how to manage small business accounting, to human resources, to investing in precious metals to how to pick stocks or plan for your financial future or buy a house

- Product/Industry Specific – think software, or a professional niche like immigration law, or small business accounting

- Political or Social commentary

- Music & Entertainment – here you can break out in to movies, or music or art, or do a compilation

- Humor or satire

- Educational – for example, on VoiceAmerica we've had shows about training animals, the Civil War and other niche topics

- Advice – dating, relationships, parenting, finding a better job, building a career, organizing your life, etc.

- Self Help or Life Coaching – this is a big one and also allows for a lot of flexibility in terms of episode by episode topicality

- Something beyond – think conspiracy theories, or UFOs or an analysis of the Mayan Calendar

- Spiritual – and this doesn't necessarily have to be "church on Sunday"

- Ethnic or Regional – why not have a show about everything Irish or Indian or Icelandic (or alliteration for that matter!). What about a show where you only talked about things in Arizona, or exploring California, or great places in New York?

- Travel, Leisure or Hobbies

- Gossip or Conspiracy

- Sports – and I don't mean ESPN, although at VoiceAmerica we've had plenty of "all sports, all the time" type shows, but what about kayaking, or trekking or windsurfing or something that has a following, that you enjoy, but isn't being served in the marketplace

Again, there is no reason why you couldn't combine several of these into one "variety" show. That variety could end up being "Extreme Sports" or "Music and Movies", we'll talk about how to break up the show "clock" in Chapter 6.

2. **Make a Quick Initial "Show Clock"** that outlines some of the basic components and objectives of your show. Are you going to have guests? Are you looking for sponsors or advertisers? What is the basic goal of your show? What products or services of your own are you going to promote? These are just a few of the questions that we will cover in later chapters, but it's a good idea to make a quick roadmap when getting started.

3. **Make a Tentative Show Calendar** which outlines topics or guests that you want or already know.

· · · · ·

How Defining the Right Message Defined One Man's Future

You've heard the story about finding a needle in a haystack right? It's impossible, right? Well here's what I learned from a man we'll call "Joe" about needles and haystacks. Joe was an old school, set in stone financial planner, and quite successful in his own right. When it came to advertising and marketing it was direct mail, chambers of commerce meetings, grin and grips and referrals. The radio was something he listened to in the car for weather and news on his drive into the office. In early 2001, the Internet and RADIO together was completely foreign to him, and pretty much everyone else. It was new territory.

At first wrapping his head around broadcast media looked like it wasn't going to happen. But being a traditional guy, he wasn't going to let it go until it was exhausted.

We went through his entire repertoire and history of success as a financial advisor and almost every financial instrument and discipline he could think of…and trust me I learned a lot about finance from Joe.

After sharing some concepts with Joe, listening to his goals and then shifting to what he would want to listen to on a radio show, Joe had an epiphany. The broadcast media "light bulb" went off!

He figured out that the best way to find the needle in the haystack was to BURN IT DOWN!

Joe jumped in with both feet and we started working to put together a Financial Show that would meet Joe's goals and create interesting and useful programming for his listeners. After several exercises Joe was on fire and ready to get started broadcasting.

His message wasn't closing new clients, or pure braggadocio or even being the smartest guy in the room.

His message was simple **"It's not how much you make, it's how much you keep".**

After tussling around in the haystack of who, what, where and why, Joe defined his message in a simple way. If you want the best clients, give the best advice, and start simple. For Joe his ideal client was one that was his for life, and their kids, and their grandkids. So educating his audience on how to preserve the bounty of their efforts was the logical place to start.

After his first two years broadcasting with VoiceAmerica Joe's life significantly changed. Not only was he the most talked about individual at industry and community events, he authored two books which became successful in their own right. Without planning his show and taking the plunge Joe might not have found the creative inspiration to write these books, become a leader in his community and improve his station in life.

It was all new then, not just for Joe, but for Internet Talk Radio as well. Joe did have an epiphany and defined his message, audience and goals almost simultaneously. In Chapter 2 I'll get into Defining Your Audience in more depth and Chapter 4 we'll talk about Defining Your Goals. But Joe set the standard for Step 1 – Defining Your Message.

At VoiceAmerica we start all of our new hosts on a 13 week pilot program to help them find their voice and get the format of their show exactly how they want it. Joe was fond of closing his show with "If it worked for me, it can work for you". Wisdom at the bottom of a burnt down haystack!

· · · · ·

Get the up to date worksheets at www.jeffspenard.com and other tools for planning, producing and promoting your show. They're FREE, they just keep getting better with each new show and idea.

CHAPTER 2
DEFINING YOUR AUDIENCE

Our basic need for approval dictates that EVERYONE needs to hear what we have to say!

The United Nations Department of Economic and Social Affairs estimates that the Global Population is 7.2 Billion.

That's a lot of potential listeners!

So when you step back from that ledge and get real about who might potentially listen to your show that number gets a little smaller.

The most important step in defining your audience is breaking it down to the value of an individual listener (and of course, to you!

So here's the exercise.

1. **What do you want them to do for you?**

   This doesn't necessarily fall under an all in one size fits all answer. Depending upon the topic of your show, you might have a variety of goals for your listeners.

   (a) Buy books – your book or your guest's books (if you have a website and an Amazon Associates account, you can make a little bit of money selling books while promoting them). It's important to note here that if it's "your book" it doesn't necessarily even have to be a "published" book in the traditional sense. It could be a downloadable PDF that is maybe 20 pages, or a study or white paper. Get them to register their name and email at least to get the free download.

   (b) Buy products – yours or your guest's. It's important to note here that the products must be easily purchased, either by phone or through an online shopping cart that you own, or even Amazon.

   (c) A call to action – this would be a good one for a political or social issue show. It could be make a donation, join the party, contact an elected official, fill out an online petition, etc. There are a lot of possibilities for calls to action.

(d) Discussion – listener participation can sometime be difficult to achieve as many people listen on their mobile device, and also listen to archived/on demand shows versus the live broadcast. Encouraging email or Facebook questions is becoming a better way to engage the audience in discussion, even if you don't have the "questioner" live on the broadcast.

(e) Join your email or mobile list – this one should be a given not only for your radio show, but for just about everything you do!

(f) Redeem a discount code – everyone loves discount codes, why not incorporate one into your show.

(g) Register for a free consultation, just like a discount code, everyone likes something for free. Even lawyers use the 30 minute free consultation to determine if there is a fit for their services.

2. **What do they gain from listening to you?**
   a. Answers to their questions
   b. Discussion
   c. Interesting Guests
   d. Provocative Topics
   e. Discount codes or offers

f. Entertainment

g. Inspiration

3. **Do they have a geographic profile?**

For the most part you are broadcasting to a global audience, however, there are plenty of examples of a show targeting a specific geographic audience. A Chamber of Commerce or local, state or regional organization such as a non-profit or political organization would be good examples.

4. **Do they have an economic profile?**

In most cases a listener's economic profile doesn't apply. However, financial shows as an example definitely have an economic profile. Are you targeting high net worth individuals, real estate investors, hedge fund managers, or just the average Joe with his day to day operations.

5. **Do they have a specific need for information?**

In general the answer to this question is "yes" otherwise they wouldn't be listening! As you are planning guests, structuring your show and considering sponsorship swhat is the information required to make the process work for you and the sponsor? Asking this question is a requirement. For example, a technology show could be a full hour discussion on a specific application, or it could be broken up into 4 segments covering 4 separate new products as they hit the market. It really depends on how you have defined your audience.

As I mentioned at the beginning of this chapter, it's your show and it's quite possible that your audience will be a combo platter of several different listener profiles, objectives and goals.

As your show progresses you will probably change up the format a little bit, add new features and learn more about your audience demographics.

· · · · ·

A Celebrated Sportscaster "Picks His Audience"

Some of you may have heard of a gentleman by the name of Pat Summerall? After decades of big network commentary talking to a sports audience around the world this gentleman was looking to build an audience of his own.

Pat not only was a professional athlete but was most recognized after the game as a sports journalist and broadcast commentator for the NFL on major networks such as NBC, ABC and CBS and down the road ESPN and Fox Sports.

Summerall began his football career playing for the Arkansas Razorbacks. After college Summerall was drafted in 1952 to the Detroit Lions going on to play for the St. Louis Cardinals, and the New York Giants during which he played in The Greatest Game Ever Played. It was his game winning field goal for the Giants against the Cleveland Browns that lead up to the contest against the Colts. At 49 yards his field goal on the final play of the game was the longest completion of the entire season.

Pat and I got to know each other back in the mid 2000's when VoiceAmerica decided to expand our talk format and introduce VoiceAmericaSports to the world.

Summerall already had a rich history and a full life not only with his family, but also the athletic community.

Growing up playing many sports namely football, tennis, baseball and basketball. Summerall was destined for a career doing what he loved, sports.

In total, Pat Summerall announced 16 Super Bowls on network television (more than any other announcer), 26 Masters Tournaments, and 21 US Opens. He also contributed to 10 Super Bowl broadcasts on CBS Radio as a pregame host or analyst.

At the time I was working with Ray Ellis former Philadelphia Eagle and then sports channel director for VoiceAmerica

Sports. We were looking to expand our format and put several new shows together when we started talking to Pat Summerall.

After several phone conversations and a trip to Dallas to go meet Pat at his home we spent many hours talking about what soon became *"The Pat Summerall Show"*.

What became apparent was the importance to Pat that he would now have control of his own content and the syndication rights and copyrights of the show. After being a network broadcaster for decades doing it for the love of the game, and I would imagine the pay wasn't so bad either, but never really controlling (owning) the content that was being televised to the hundreds of thousands of viewers around the world was something missing for Pat.

Now the biggest thing was Pat was going to be able to build an audience that was all his own. He controlled the content, he had any guest on the show that he wanted and he was able to make all decisions that would determine how he would build his audience.

Unfortunately, Pat passed in 2013 and he is missed by millions. I treasure the time I spent with Pat and the lessons that we learned together. The most important being, love what you do, try to do it well and you will find an audience.

• • • • •

Get the up to date worksheets at www.jeffspenard.com and other tools for planning, producing and promoting your show. They're FREE, they just keep getting better with each new show and idea.

CHƆPTƐR 3
CHOOSING YOUR MEDIUM: RADIO OR TV

There is an old joke in the media business "You have a face for radio"!

Depending upon your preferences for being behind a microphone or in front of a camera there are several different options for both radio and tv broadcasting. There is really no reason that you can't do both simultaneously similar to a Rush Limbaugh or Alex Jones or other broadcaster that utilizes both terrestrial and internet broadcasting for radio and TV simultaneously. For our purposes, we'll be focusing on internet and related delivery technologies (i.e. mobile and tablet).

Internet Talk Radio

Currently, 47% of all Americans ages 12 and older -- an estimated 124 million people -- said they have listened to online radio in the last month, while 36% (94 million people) have listened in the last week. These figures are up from 45% and 33%, respectively, in 2013. The average amount of time spent listening increased from 11 hours, 56 minutes per week in 2013 to 13 hours 19 minutes in 2014.

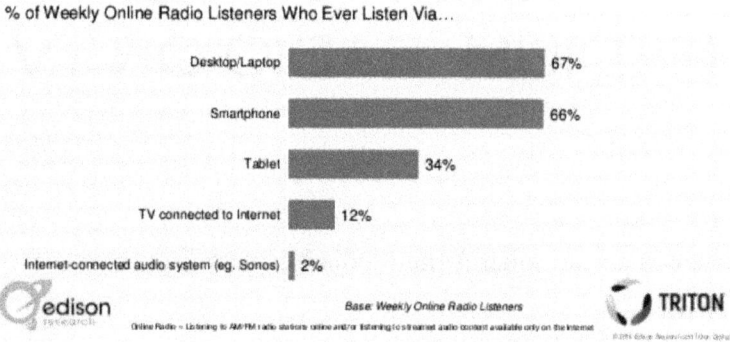

% of Weekly Online Radio Listeners Who Ever Listen Via...

Desktop/Laptop	67%
Smartphone	66%
Tablet	34%
TV connected to Internet	12%
Internet-connected audio system (eg. Sonos)	2%

edison

Base: Weekly Online Radio Listeners

TRITON

Online Radio = Listening to AM/FM radio stations online and/or listening to streamed audio content available only on the Internet

Online radio is making big gains in audience share, with Pandora leading the way, according to the latest figures from Edison Research and Triton Digital, published in the annual "Infinite Dial" report, based on a national survey of 2,023 people conducted in February.

As might be expected, usage numbers are much higher for teens and younger adults, with 75% of Americans ages 12-24 listening to online radio in the last month, compared to 50% of Americans ages 25-54 and 21% of Americans 55+. The weekly figures for the same age groups were 64%, 37% and 13%, respectively.

Of special note for advertisers: 75% of respondents who listen to online radio on a weekly basis said commercials are a fair price to pay for free programming -- roughly comparable to 80% for weekly AM/FM listeners. In fact, online audio ads were viewed as less annoying than broadcast counterparts, with 47% saying AM/FM radio ads are more intrusive, versus 30% for Internet audio ads.

Turning to specific platforms, 31% listened to Pandora in the last month, and 22% in the last week. For Clear Channel's iHeartRadio, the monthly and weekly figures are 9% and 5%, respectively. Apple's new iTunes Radio, launched in the second half of 2013, is off to a good start with 8% of Americans age 12 and up listening in the last month, while Spotify garnered 6%.

Turning to other formats, 15% of Americans ages 12 and up now listen to podcasts, up from 12% in 2013.

No surprise – smartphones loom large in the latest research: 61% of Americans ages 12 and up now own a smartphone, increasing to 80% among adults ages 18-34. This is enabling a whole range of associated behaviors, such as in-car listening: 26% of mobile phone users are connecting devices to vehicles to listen to digital audio, including Bluetooth links, up from 21% last in 2013. The proportion rises to 43% of Americans ages 12-24 (compared to 27% of Americans ages 25-54 and 10% of Americans 55+). Overall, 66% of online radio listeners say they tune in via their smartphone.

Although digital is growing fast, broadcast radio still dominates overall audio consumption -- with 75% of consumers saying they turn to broadcast stations to discover new music, versus just 48% for Pandora. Broadcast also prevails in in-car listening, with 58% of respondents saying they listen to AM/ FM "almost all of the time" or "most of the time," versus just 6% for online radio.

US Monthly Digital Radio Listeners, 2012-2018	2012	2013	2014	2015	2016	2017	2018
Monthly digital radio listeners (millions)	132.5	147.8	159.8	169.3	175.8	180.0	183.4
—% change		17.3%	11.5%	8.1%	5.9%	3.9%	2.4%	1.9%
—% of internet users		55.8%	60.1%	63.5%	66.0%	67.4%	68.0%	68.4%
—% of population		42.2%	46.7%	50.1%	52.7%	54.3%	55.2%	55.8%

Note: internet users of any age who have listened to digital broadcasts of terrestrial radio stations, digital-only radio stations or audio podcasts via any device at least once per month
Source: eMarketer, Feb 2014

168354   www.eMarketer.com

Internet TV

Internet TV goes far beyond simple streaming video such as YouTube or Vimeo, but that is a good place to start, and we'll address those mass platforms later as part of the marketing strategy for your true broadcast platform.

Back in the day, and not too long ago, it would require hundreds of millions of dollars to create a broadcast network.

This is still true when it comes to broadcast or cable television, which still holds a tremendous audience.

However, that audience is differentiating its taste in "mediums" – the method that information is delivered to them.

As traditional TV time declines, digital video viewing across devices is driving time spent with video as a whole. Research released by UBS in April 2015 highlighted a leap in digital video viewership last year and also pointed to a declining traditional TV audience. The source estimated that US digital video viewership rose 32% quarter over quarter in Q1 2015, compared with a decline of 4% for TV viewers—both trends that had accelerated since Q4 2014.

Attitudes Toward Original Digital Video (ODV) Programming/Content* Among US Buy-Side Professionals, April 2015

% of respondents

	Agree completely	Somewhat agree	Total
I would be more likely to place ads on ODV programming if there were research that proved it works as well or better than TV ads at generating sales	31%	44%	75%
I would be more likely to place ads on ODV programming if there were research that proved it works as well or better than TV ads at branding	28%	47%	75%
Having digital metrics that are consistent with TV would increase the amount of dollars allocated to ads on ODV programming	24%	48%	72%
ODV programming is compelling	22%	50%	72%
ODV programming will begin to become as important as TV programming in the next 3-5 years	30%	37%	67%
ODV programming will begin to become as important as original TV programming, but it will take more than 5 years	25%	41%	66%
I would spend more advertising on ODV programming if I could buy it more like TV ads	22%	43%	65%
I would spend more advertising on ODV programming if there were more consistency in ad formats across sites so I could buy scale	21%	44%	65%

Note: n=305; reflects responses of 4 or 5 on a 5-point scale; *programming (not advertising) that is professionally produced specifically for digital consumption
Source: Interactive Advertising Bureau (IAB), "Digital Content NewFronts: Digital Video Spend Study" conducted by Advertiser Perceptions, April 27, 2015

189227   www.eMarketer.com

The shift in consumption is spurring changes in how advertisers approach video placements, and April 2015 polling by Advertiser Perceptions for the Interactive Advertising Bureau (IAB) found that 67% of US agencies and marketers were moving funds away from TV toward digital video advertising. Respondents were particularly interested in original digital video (ODV) programming, which had increased its share of digital video spending steadily over the past three years, from 34% in 2013 to 40% in 2015.

Advertisers were once again most likely to take dollars from TV to put toward ODV, cited by 75%. And their outlook on the industry supports their reason for doing so. More than two-thirds of buy-side professionals agreed that ODV programming would become as important as TV in the next three to five years; a similar percentage felt the same in terms of importance, but believed the change was further out.

In order for ODV to bring in the bucks and rise to the same level of importance as TV, responses indicated that providers will need to present research that demonstrates the content's effectiveness at generating sales and brand awareness. Creating digital metrics the same as those used for television and mimicking the ad-buying process of TV ads could also help boost growth, along with consistency in ad formats.

Obstacles to Spending More on Original Digital Video (ODV) Advertising* According to US Marketers vs. Agency Professionals, April 2015
% of respondents

	Marketers	Agency professionals
ROI vs. other media	54%	37%
Quality of content	45%	39%
Audience and campaign measurement	41%	38%
Price	39%	46%
Viewability	36%	37%
Scale	32%	29%
Video ad unit lengths	30%	18%
Complexity of executing a buy	26%	18%
Lack of transparency in the buying process	25%	24%
Lack of promotion of the video content to audiences	24%	27%
Clients' lack of understanding of the space	-	33%
Other	1%	1%
No hurdles	4%	3%

Note: n=305; *e.g., the type of video presented at the NewFronts
Source: Interactive Advertising Bureau (IAB), "Digital Content NewFronts: Digital Video Spend Study" conducted by Advertiser Perceptions, April 27, 2015

189228   www.eMarketer.com

The lack of certain metrics—specifically return on investment vs. other media, audience and campaign measurement and viewability—were key obstacles preventing respondents from moving more spending to original digital video ads, further supporting the need for research that lays out hard numbers. Pricing was another top challenge—and one that could be solved if advertisers have the figures to back up their desire to up ODV placements.

For ODV to join the ranks of TV in terms of importance, services will need to present advertisers with research and metrics that prove it's worth the dollars.- See more at: http://www.emarketer.com/Article/Advertisers-Focus-on-Original-Digital-Video-Programming/1012430/9#sthash. rrkUMNui.dpuf

· · · · ·

Sometimes The Medium Chooses You

Choosing your medium TV or radio that is the question! I work with many different clients that have content that supports both radio and TV. The decision to broadcast one way or the other really depends on the type of content that you are looking share.

Johnny is a good example of a man that does both radio and television with me. Johnny has quite a professional background in media being commentator on Fox News, CBS, ABC, MSNBC, CNBC among others. You can read his articles and learn about him in *The Wall Street Journal, The New York Times, Forbes* and *USA Today*. Johnny has developed extensive programming on VoiceAmerica Radio and VoiceAmerica TV.

For nearly 10 years Johnny and I have worked together developing and producing his radio show on the VoiceAmerica

Business Channel. His show is built around his proven system of helping clients invest their capital and the best ways to handle their money.

After years of success on the radio, Johnny I started talking about creating a television channel that focused on interviewing some of the top CEOs that he had as guests on his radio show. We started by planning the show and took the idea to a storyboard then to reality.

The choice to do TV in addition to radio was because Johnny realized the benefit of him doing one on one with top CEOs across the country on TV. As CEOs often don't have the time for a full half hour or hour segment on his radio show, we created a different format to meet their time schedule, as well as to match the shorter viewing patterns of the online TV audience.

We started putting together 8 to 12 minute segments of one-on-one interviews with Johnny on Wall Street and placed them on the CEO channel on VoiceAmerica.TV. A little secret for those of you reading this book Johnny was able to **charge a couple of thousand dollars for each of these CEO's** to do these interviews with him and then provided the CEOs with digital copies for use on their sites and social media. So not only was it additional content provided about him to a new audience, but it was also an opportunity for Johnny to make some money at the same time.

· · · · ·

Get the up to date worksheets at www.jeffspenard.com and other tools for planning, producing and promoting your show. They're FREE, they just keep getting better with each new show and idea.

CHAPTER 4
DEFINING YOUR GOALS

This is where is gets a little tricky! What do YOU want to accomplish by broadcasting your messaging to potentially millions of people?

The answer to this question is quite different for every person or organization looking to broadcast their message on radio or TV. Some of this is defined by your existing or potential audience. Some of this definition will probably change as you get further down the road in your broadcasting "career".

Over the years we at VoiceAmerica have seen talk radio and TV used in a variety of creative ways. Here are some of the most popular.

1. **Industry Leadership** – many of our hosts, already thought leaders in their specific industries, use their show to bolster that image and expand their industry leadership position and credibility.

2. **Connections** – one very common utilization of a talk radio show is simply to get in the door to connections a host might not otherwise have access to without a show. Everyone likes attention, and inviting them to be a guest on your radio show offers a different level of access to potential partners or customers that you might not have had before.

3. **Credibility** – a talk radio or TV show provides a certain level of credibility that you might not have had without one. In the world of new media, talk radio and TV offer a higher level of credibility versus simply talking over some graphics and posting to YouTube or Vimeo.

4. **Support for a Project** – many hosts are also authors or involved in a non-profit or issue based project and find that talk radio or TV provide a more "interactive explanation" than simply a website or blog.

5. **Support of a Product** – we've seen a lot of success in a variety of industries whereby a talk radio show is ideal for support of a product, the software industry is a perfect example of this type of support.

6. **Fun** – never underestimate the amount of fun you can have with a little bit of work on hosting your own radio or TV show.

· · · · ·

How an Investment in Yourself Can Turn Into a Goldmine

"Roger", a fourth generation wealth management expert, decided to produce a radio show entitled "3 Different Ways to Calculate Wealth". Roger had big goals for the show. This was a man driven to really reach people to teach his style of wealth management which he called 3 Dimensional Wealth. His system encompasses Financial Wealth, Personal Wealth, and Social Wealth.

I remember setting goals back in the early days working with Roger when we first started putting the show together. We had big goals and first he wanted to establish a national reputation in the field of finance and to become one of the leading experts in the field. His second goal was to establish a solid repeat listener base for his radio show.

About six weeks after the show launched Roger invited me to fly out to New Orleans for the Million Dollar Round Table convention. At the time this convention was one of the biggest events I had ever been to and this was the insurance gala of the year.

This is where all the money men get together in the insurance industry, share ideas, new products, regulatory changes and strategies. There are speakers, break out rooms and business happening all around you and over 1,000 exhibitors, and more than 10,000 attendees wandering the convention center floor.

This was the first time he had ever attended the Million Dollar Round Table. To differentiate his booth from the others we set up shop in his booth with our remote broadcast studio. We had a sound board, two microphones, two headsets and we turned his exhibit into an on-air studio.

I hit the floor and gathered as many speakers as I could to bring them over to sit down with Roger to do five to ten minute interviews. The reception was tremendous and Roger made a large amount of new contacts.

It went over so well that the next year when the Million Dollar Round Table came about again they asked Roger to be one of the top speakers at this gala and paid him a $10,000 fee to get up on stage and speak in front of thousands of people, goal number one accomplished!

After building a rather large audience Roger had over 30,000 listeners to his show on a monthly basis thus Goal Number 2 was accomplished.

And for the icing on the cake for Roger was the fact that when a few years had gone by the University of Buffalo decided they were going to use "3 Different Ways to Calculate Wealth" as part of their college curriculum in upstate New York.

One of the keys to the success of our strategy was the goal setting process. Setting precise goals and following that path was an integral part of Roger's success and a key contributor to the future success of "3 Different Ways to Calculate Wealth".

• • • • •

Get the up to date worksheets at www.jeffspenard.com and other tools for planning, producing and promoting your show. They're FREE, they just keep getting better with each new show and idea.

CHƆPTⱭR 5
PLANNING YOUR STRATEGY

The planning and preparation for your overall strategy is key to the success of your show. So is the strategy for each individual show, but we'll talk about that later.

Here are some steps to help develop your strategy.

It all starts with a series of outlines.

1. Radio and Television are built on 13 week quarters.

2. A list of potential topics – make a list of potential topics for each of your shows. These will inevitably change from the time you make the outline until the actual show date.

3. A list of potential guests – these should fit in with your topics, or some of my clients have chosen to ignore the "topics" and simply go straight for the guests.

4. A list of potential sponsors – most shows don't start off with sponsors right out of the gate, but it has been known to happen depending upon your reach in your community.

5. A list of your current assets (web site, blog, YouTube account, Social Media accounts like Facebook and Twitter, , email lists, customer/prospect lists, etc.)

6. Marketing strategy – we'll discuss this in more detail in future chapters. But jot down some creative ideas that might not apply simply to the internet. For example, let say you ship a physical product to your clients, consider printing up 3 to a sheet flyers for your show and including them in the shipping container, or simply adding the show name, time and web location to your signature at the bottom of your emails.

· · · · ·

Get the up to date worksheets at www.jeffspenard.com and other tools for planning, producing and promoting your show. They're FREE, they just keep getting better with each new show and idea.

CHAPTER 6
THE BASIC STRUCTURE OF A BROADCAST

It's your show, so you have some flexibility in the way you want to present it. Do you have a co-host, do you have guests, do you have two guests at the same time, do you have multiple topically differing segments, do you have regular segments, do you take calls?

Those are just some of the considerations. Here are the basics of a one hour talk show.

Plan out your show clock beforehand. Don't try to fly by the seat of your pants once you are in the studio or "live" via Skype or phone. Maybe if you're an experienced broadcaster, but even then, it's better to have a plan, especially if you're working with an engineer and with guests.

Scheduling or "blocking" out the time on your show clock in advance is a must, especially if it's your first show. Even after your first show, having a well-planned schedule will make your life easier and your show more professional. It will also help you plan for possible future sponsors or advertisers, and help you plan your questions for your guests in advance, as well as keep control of your show.

Planning before the show also makes it more difficult for you to run out of things to say and helps to avoid the evil "dead air".

If you're a beginning broadcaster don't worry if in the course of the first several shows you run under or over your show clock. If you're working with a professional engineer they will keep you on track with that "little voice in your head".

Jimmy Kimmel has a long standing joke at the end of each of his late night shows where he apologizes to Matt Damon for running out of time. There is a lesson in this.

Usually you will be under, not over, especially if you're hosting the show solo without guests. It's a good idea to have some reserve content handy just in case you're under schedule.

Make a list of things you are very familiar with and keep them by the microphone. Those topics could simply be anecdotes about your family, a business situation, a book you love or just read, or even something in the news that is pertinent to your topicality.

As your show progresses you will inevitably develop your own internal show clock. For the first several shows make written notes about how close you came to a perfect close and adjust accordingly.

Before we get to the actual show clock, let's talk about some of the key components of a show:

Intro – this is where the big voice or soothing voice or rock and roll voice comes in and announces "Get ready for the BIG BAD BOB BOBSLEDDING Show, with your host BIG BAD BOB, brought to you by the Jamaican Bobsledding team, competing since 1986. To participate email bob@ bobsledding.com, tweet #bigbadbobsled or call 1-888-555- 1212. Now here's Big Bad Bob." Preferably you have some music playing in the background that brings consistency to your show.

NOTE: be careful when using copyrighted music. You will get in trouble and have to pay royalties or fines to the music licensing bureaus. If you know an artist, get them to sign a release form like this one: www.jeffspenard/releaseform.doc

Here are some resources for cost effective "royalty free" music that you can license if you're not sure. Royalty free is defined in most cases as a one time fee for unlimited usage. Some "royalty free" sites have differing licensing guidelines based upon how you're going to use it, example, for a website or a presentation the cost might be lower than for a radio or television broadcast.

http://www.cssmusic.com/
http://www.themusicase.com/
http://ww.pond5.com/

If you're working with a professional engineer on your show, or with a company that produces this sort of audio track, they might already have a bulk library that they have available as part of the production fee.

Outro – basically the same as the intro except that it's more like "Don't go away, BIG BAD BOB will be back with more bobsled radio, send in your questions to email bob@bobsledding.com, tweet #bigbadbobsled or call 1-888-555-1212."

Then you go to commercial, or sponsors, or promotion of your website, products, book, services, whatever.

Rejoinder – this is your "Welcome back, you're listening to….".

Closer – this is the really fast thank you for listening, tune in next week, or whenever and don't forget to listen to the archives of this show on www.bigbadbobsled.com.

You "Intro" and "Closer" should always be consistent, but feel free if your budget or skill set afford to have a variety of Outro's and Rejoinders if you want to mix it up.

If you are breaking your show clock in two separate segments, or have a special "segment" after your first Outro, here is a place you could sell sponsorship.

Example: "Welcome back to the Big Bad Bobsled show and this week's SPECIAL SEGMENT brought to you by Fred's House of Bob Sleds". This also works if you just want to have two sponsors, one for each segment of the show.

Here's a sample show clock for a 60 minute show.

1 minute   –   Intro

12 minutes –   this might be a welcome and some commentary that is "just you", maybe a review of the news, a book review or just something that's on your mind to warm up the audience. This is also a good place to bombard them with your call in, tweet, web and email information.

1 minute   –   Outro

2 minutes –   Advertising or Sponsorship

1 minute   –   Rejoinder

12 minutes –   Guest #1

1 minute   –   Outro

2 minutes –   Advertising or Sponsorship

1 minute   –   Rejoinder

12 minutes –   Guest #2

1 minute   –   Outro

2 minutes –   Advertising or Sponsorship

1 minute   –   Rejoinder

6 minutes –   SPECIAL SEGMENT(s), listen mail, reviews, etc.

4 minutes –   Thanks to Guests, Advertisers, Sponsors and "warm up" for the next show.*

1 minute   –   Closer

Here are some things to ponder when setting up your show clock.

Be Consistent. Things always change and talk radio is no different. Expect your show clock to be slightly flexible. For example: normally you have two guests, but all of a sudden you've booked the President of _____ as a guest. You're going to want to just have 1 Guest on this "Special Edition" of the show.

But for the most part, talk radio listeners want to know that if they tune in at a certain time that segment will be there. This of it like you're watching the local news. They never tell you the full weather at the beginning of the news cast, it's always 5 minutes or so before the end of the news cast. It's like putting the milk at the back of the grocery store, you have to walk all the way through the store to get to the milk!

I was speaking with a friend of mine about this show clock consistency issue and he brought up how when he lived in Washington, DC he would listen to the G. Gordon Liddy Show broadcasting out of Falls Church, Virginia.

He said depending upon who the guests were, he might not tune into the "rest of the show", but he always caught the first hour, that's when Liddy "read the news".

Liddy would spend the first hour, with some advertising breaks, to essentially give about 50 minutes of the top stories from major publications (this was pre-internet news destinations). Very little commentary from Liddy, just straight news from The Wall Street Journal, The New York Times, The Washington Post, etc.

I thought that was an interesting example, especially when my friend, a conservative, told me that all of his liberal DC friends ALSO tuned in, at least for the news because it added VALUE to their listening time, and usually they would also stay tuned for the rest of show.

Guests

We'll talk more about guests in Chapter 8, but this is a good place to get that discussion started.

"New Guests" provide fresh content and perspective to your show, along with hopefully bringing new listeners.

"Old Guests" that are popular (or even better, sponsors) can add consistent value to your show with segments or snippets that might only be 3-5 minutes per show. Never underestimate your guest's following, and always allow them to promote their own "thing" in exchange for their time or money.

Listener Calls, Emails, Tweets, Etc.

Engaging your audience on air, social media or by email is a great way to keep the flow going and build your audience.

If you have a call in number, plaster it everywhere. You might also consider using Skype for your call ins, or encourage your audience to ask questions via chat using a chat program, Skype, or even Facebook (a good way to get "friends").

If you're just starting off your show you might want to plant a couple of callers. Sounds sneaky, but until you've established a regular audience that feels "comfortable" calling in don't expect the phones to be ringing off the hook. Booking great guests helps with this problem.

Keep in mind that with today's listening audience not just sitting around the radio, but mobile, in the car, in the office, and more importantly, **on demand** as a download they can listen to at their leisure, your audience might not be in the right place at the right time to call.

However, they can send in emails or tweet using a hashtag.

If you watch the news, or even The Daily Show, they are constantly asking their audience to tweet or email in their questions or comments, and **ALWAYS** at the end of the show for the next day's broadcast.

This is also a good place to be CONSTANT again.

Example: On *The Nightly Show with Larry Wilmore* on Comedy Central his audience participation builder is a question he answers from an audience member at the end of every show. They Tweet in their question using hashtag #Keepit100. The questions are sometimes serious, but his answers are usually pretty silly, but it's something that the audience knows is going to be there at the end of EVERY SHOW.

Especially if you are taking questions or comments via social media or email, make sure to always send a personal thank you, and mention them on the air by name and location if you have it. Depending upon your show's topicality you might choose to use first name and last initial, or just their internet "handle" if you have it.

One thing to watch out with callers.

Know how to shut off a caller quickly. Even if you have a screener working your phones, they will still slip by with something. If you're familiar with Howard Stern you will know of the enormous amounts of BABBABOEY prank calls that were made from his audience to OTHER SHOWS.

If you are working with a professional firm they will probably have a few second delay on their system which will help cut prank callers or other pests off before they "get you".

Dead Air

We all know what dead air is and how embarrassed we feel for the host when that uncomfortable silence happens. AVOID IT! Keep something handy to switch to, or even some music around in case something happens and you need a moment to recover.

• • • • •

A Great Broadcast is Like a Good Workout Routine

If you wanted to talk about a nutritional front man, NO ONE ever beat Jack LaLanne. Not even at 80 years old could anything stop Jack!!!

Most of you know who Jack LaLanne was. If you don't, let me introduce him to you. Here is a gentleman whose life was run by nutritional facts and of course the Jack LaLanne Juicer.

Jack loved the concept of having his own show to go beyond what he could do in short snippets on TV and to interact with his loyal followers and fans. Jack had always been a front man for nutrition and fitness, and was considered the "Godfather of Fitness". He held the world record with 1,063 pushups in

23 minutes, he swam the length of the Golden Gate Bridge in San Francisco Bay with 140 pounds of weights tied to him at 40, at 61 he did it AGAIN with the 1,000 pounds at 70 he swam a mile towing 75 row boats with people in them! The man was a force of nature. A nature he created for himself with discipline, planning and a love for living. He approached his radio show the same way.

With thousands of guest appearances and interviews Jack was pretty much a household name. But he never really had his own nutritional program where he could really speak directly to those he spent his life helping live better, feel better and be happier and healthier.

The greatest part of Jack's show, and this starts off just like all of our other shows with a 13-week pilot series, was that Jack decided to make the show a family affair.

Jack was a huge family guy and once he realized that he had total creative freedom he was elated to bring his wife Shirley and his son Jon to be part of the show.

After working with Jack for over two years I learned some lessons. Not just about being healthy, but about stability, routine and discipline. I found out that that Jack would run five times around his own facility in California – about a 1 mile length for each lap he ran around his corporate office. Everyday Jack would start with a five mile run around his facilities.

He was a guy that was so smooth to work with, so excited about being alive, and such a professional about everything he did, it was like working with a little kid on Christmas Day each and every week to do his new radio show. He was the epitome of constant improvement in everything he did.

Jack's show became one of our most audience driven shows. Tons of phone calls, lots of emails, lots of participation, and an explosive listener base growth trajectory. Jack had that kind of personality that just drew people in. You couldn't help but be engaged and even for those few moments that you had with him, be inspired you to live a better life.

Working with Jack taught me a lot about working with people. About how a positive personality is infectious. Jack taught me a lot about setting goals and methodically working to achieve them. He approached life with gusto and always stuck to his plan. Planning was part of his roadmap to success. Not just for fitness, not just for being a great husband, father and mentor to countless millions, but even with his approach to his show.

Working with Jack was a true learning experience. I learned more about myself by working with him, God rest his soul, than possibly with anyone I've ever met. Nothing stopped then man, he was consistently working to improve himself, the people around him and the world in general. His ability to adapt and grow and learn was one of the things that made his show so great. It evolved with him.

Unfortunately, Jack passed at 93. He had a series of great quotations about healthy living. One of them included an analogy to bank accounts and your health.

"The more you put in, the more you can take out." Jack understood and lived a philosophy of continuous improvement. Like life, relationships and your bank account, a properly fed, nourished and "exercised" radio show can live on FOREVER and just get better every day!

We all miss Jack. He was one of the greats.

· · · · ·

Get the up to date worksheets at www.jeffspenard.com and other tools for planning, producing and promoting your show. They're FREE, they just keep getting better with each new show and idea.

CHAPTER 7
PREPARING YOUR BROADCAST TOOLKIT

Although it's not completely necessary, over the past 20 years we've learned that one of the keys to a successful talk show is being prepared. This goes not only for you, but also for your guest. Here are some ideas for tools and how to use them.

Media Kit

A Media Kit is important especially if you're going to seek sponsors or selling advertising. It's also helpful when going after high profile guests that you don't have a previous relationship. It can be as simple as a one pager with your bio information, network information, show information and maybe a roster of past or future guests.

As your show evolves it may become much more complex with listener numbers (once you have them), an outline of your website for advertising, a rate card for audio ads, etc. It sounds a bit silly, but include ALL of your contact information – Name, email, website, phone, fax, Facebook, Twitter, Show Page, etc. You would be surprised at how many people leave off their contact information.

Press Release Kit

In Chapter 10 I get more in depth about press releases. The same Sample there would be applicable to using with your Guests if you want to put out press releases for upcoming shows.

Some guests might want to put out their own press releases to promote themselves, or their product/service, or book, etc. Giving them a template to work with makes it easier for them and ensures that you will get the links back to your website and Show Page that will help you build traffic and audience.

Openers, Closers, Rejoinders, etc.

As I discussed in Chapter 6 to make your show sound professional you'll want Openers, Closers, Rejoinders, and some promos for your show prepared in advance. The promos especially can be used as a marketing tool, not only by yourself, but also by your guests.

Guest Checklist

Just to keep everything organized it's a good idea to put together a Guest Checklist for yourself. Something like this.

1. Guest Information Form Sent
2. Guest Instructions Form Sent
3. Press Release Kit Sent
4. Press Release Written
5. Press Release Submitted
6. Social Media Promotion
7. Media Kit Sent
8. Website/Blog Promotion

You might even consider making up a form that has Sent and Received Columns that you print out and actually check the boxes, or put it in a spreadsheet if you are so inclined.

Guest Interview Form

Depending upon what your per show marketing strategy is you're going to need to collect some information from your guests. Many guests will simply direct you to their LinkedIn page or send you a copy of their resume. But many will take the time to fill out your form, which will save you some time in preparation.

Of course, you could always provide that as part of your "package" if you're charging for airtime. Their corporate, and possibly personal websites might also have a wealth of information about them that might not appear on a resume. Here's a basic list of what you would want to put together.

1. Name (how they want you to refer to them on the show, Dr. Robert Thaddeus Smith might want to be called Dr. Robert for example.

2. Contact information for you to promote on the show, this could be their phone number, their website, their blog or an event or book they are promoting.

3. Questionnaire – it's a good idea to ask the guest to come up with some questions they would like to be asked on the show. This helps you avoid dead air, makes them happy and save you some time doing the research. It also helps you keep the show on track and avoiding it ending up either being 100% you talking, or 100% them talking!

4. A short bio that you can use to introduce them, as well as include in any promotional graphics (like the one below) that we create for all of our hosts for email promotion, social media promotion and anywhere a graphic is important.

Guest Instructions

At VoiceAmerica we use a Skype platform for connecting our hosts, their guests and our broadcast platform because of the quality, the portability, and the cost effective nature of its ability to connect the host and guest together to generate the broadcast. It's especially convenient for our hosts who travel a lot, they can broadcast from anywhere.

Regardless of how you connect with your guests, it's a good idea to provide them with "instructions".

They'll need information about the show time and where to listen, where to listen to the archive, proper hashtags so they can promote the show on their social media, listener call in lines, etc.

Most importantly, they'll need to know how to call in to the show engineer to connect the two of you.

It's not a bad idea to send this information to them twice, once about a week or two before the show air date, and then again the day before the show, especially if you book your guests weeks or months in advance.

Get the up to date worksheets at www.jeffspenard.com and other tools for planning, producing and promoting your show. They're FREE, they just keep getting better with each new show and idea.

• • • • •

A Broadcast Toolkit is Valuable When You Are Working with a 24 Hour Day!

Some of you may know this next person, the Good Doctor, I had worked with him for several years before we really started to take off. Here is a gentleman who has written several best-selling books, made many guest appearances, and even appeared in a movie or two here and there. With over 14 million books sold and millions of enthralled movie viewers the Good Doctor became one of the first clients ever to create a multimedia platform with VoiceAmerica. You know him from the book about men and women from different planets. The movie I refer to of course is a "Secret"! A whole generation was so moved and motivated that it created a new segment of visionaries and thought leaders.

With the Good Doctor it all started with a 13 week pilot series. Within a few months we realized there was much more to offer.

The Good Doctor became the first client and our beta test to build the very first platform that included Radio, TV, Book sales, relationship consultations, speaking engagements and an ecommerce site to book and sell all of the Good Doctor's products and services under what we called at the time was our BoomBox Player.

We created a one stop shop that could embed the player on any desktop or digital device with one click of a button.

The Good Doctor was the first client to reach the 1 million viewer mark, and more importantly for the first time in his career, he owned his content 100% right down to final approval on advertisers and sponsors and all of his rich media content. He mentioned to me that he finally felt free.

As I mentioned earlier this show started with our normal 13-week pilot series. When started doing live radio the Good Doctor would do the show from his home in California, while his Co Host would be here in Phoenix Arizona.

Within 3 months of the launch, the Good Doctor decided he wanted more girth and gallantry for his show. Of course Voice America had the capability to give more with a little creativity and kibitzing.

So we set up a one camera shoot in the middle of the Good Doctor's dining room. The Doc has a beautiful home in California that was the perfect backdrop.

The show would become a 2 hour program broadcast live via radio and internet television. But the real beauty of the exercise was not just our forward looking embrace of new technology, but the consideration of the Good Doctor's fans, family and frequent listeners and their ability to not only LISTEN, but

SEE him not just live, but at their convenience and over any device. The feedback from the audience was over the top. We had succeeded!

When the Good Doctor and I were speaking month's after the champagne was gone, he mentioned to me that the reason why he was confident enough to take that leap of faith was simply because we had sat down and created not just a plan, but a tool-kit for those working with us. We were all on the same page. It was a great team effort.

· · · · ·

Get the up to date worksheets at www.jeffspenard.com and other tools for planning, producing and promoting your show. They're FREE, they just keep getting better with each new show and idea.

CHAPTER 8
HOW TO FIND GUESTS THAT BUILD YOUR AUDIENCE

So now you've chosen your platform, laid out a strategy to begin broadcasting and marketing your show, let's talk about booking guests and leveraging their existing audience to broaden your reach and appeal.

Once you've launched your show you will more than likely begin to receive copies of new books and requests from potential guests seeking publicity. You don't have to take everybody that sends you a request. Keep in mind, it's your show, and although it is a little bit of an ego boost to feel popular, it's important to weigh the value of your guest to your audience, your personal self-interest and to your overall marketing strategy.

Help A Reporter

http://www.helpareporter.com – acquired by VOCUS in 2010, Help a Reporter Out (HARO) brings 100,000 news sources, 30,000 bloggers and journalists and thousands of businesses and brands together multiple times per day via email and SMS to connect "sources" with the "story creators".

HARO is advertising supported, so it's free for you to post up an advertisement for a "show topic" that you might be considering broadcasting. You want to sign up as a "reporter" http://www.helpareporter.com/reporters in order to take advantage of the free aspect of their service. It's important that you remember that as a Radio or TV Show Host you are effectively a journalist.

Example: You want to do a story about Small Business Tax Strategies for your Business Based Talk Radio Show. Your ad might read:

"Internet Talk Radio Show focused on Business seeks professionals and business owners with experience and advice regarding small business tax strategies ranging from payroll taxes to compensation plans to establishing health care plans under new Federal regulations."

Again, HARO is free for you as a journalist and talk radio or TV broadcaster. They provide you with a blind email address so that potential guests or contributors won't have access to your identity or email address, unless you provide the name of your show or blog. This is helpful in weeding out the content that you aren't interested in hosting on your show, as well as potential solicitations that might come over the transom.

HARO has a free basic package for you as a "Source", so for your business or your book, or your services, signing up for one of their packages might also be a cost effective way to promote your brand, as well as your show. They have packages that start at $19 per month, and provide you with a profile and links to your website, etc. which is also helpful in promoting yourself and websites across the search engines. In additional journalists and media outlet such as FOX, Gannett, CNN and others utilize the HARO database when faced with a deadline or preparing a story.

Contact Any Celebrity

http://contactanycelebrity.com/ – this private database includes 60,000 verified celebrity contacts, over 7,000 companies and 13,000 representatives. It's cost effective as well. In addition, they also publish an annual hard cover version of their list for $39.95 that is available on Amazon.

Their online accessible database is equally favorably priced and is updated on a consistent basis.

http://www.specialguests.com – a free database with sum-maries of topical and in most cases current events based potential guests, authors and thought leaders.

http://www.radioguestlist.com – a booking service whereby you can submit booking requests, browse through their list and sign up for a free email notification service when new guests are announced.

http://imdb.com – the Internet Movie Database, owned by Amazon, has a comprehensive database of movie and televi-sion actors, directors, producers

http://amazon.com – a little trickier to find contact infor-mation, but with a little Google research you can find the contact information for the authors of topical books that are almost always happy to be on a talk radio show to promote themselves.

Researching Guests Audience Potential

One of the key things to selecting guests for your broadcast is computing what is the true potential value they bring to the table, other than their sagacious commentary and wisdom.

There are several obvious ways to get a handle on a guest's audience potential.

1. LinkedIn – check and see if they are 500+

2. Facebook – check their friends and their likes

3. Twitter – check their followers

4. The "obvious" – if they have a New York Times Bestseller, or are a movie star or director or a sports figure or famous musician or popular politician, obviously they are going to attract an audience, especially if you encourage them to promote the show to their existing audience via email, social media, their website, etc.

Get the up to date worksheets at www.jeffspenard.com and other tools for planning, producing and promoting your show. They're FREE, they just keep getting better with each new show and idea.

• • • • •

Finding the Right Guests in Your Own Backyard

One of the success stories that I'm most from of is a major SaaS provider. You probably use them at your office.

A company that is plastered all over the professional sports industry with commercials during Super Bowl, top shelf sponsoring of the NHL channel and developing the world's leading technology SaaS software suite.

You would think that a multi-billion technology company would just buy ads on TV for exposure.

Not the case here. The audience runs this show. In fact, the audience runs 3 shows. Here's where a host went way outside the box and put the listeners first.

What started out three or four years ago with the now famous (in the book) 13 week pilot series. The show took on a life of its own and multiplied like a paramecium!

I'm sure you guys can see a pattern when I say 13 weeks! That's how we start all of our shows. However with this Fortune 50 company what started off as a 13-week pilot series turned into a whole block of programs and just kept growing.

In total I believe we've produced over 19 individual programs for our Fortune 50 friend. The show's host is such a seasoned pro and a huge asset to her employer, and to VoiceAmerica that adding new vertical markets, new technology segments and the resulting high standard of quality programming is nearly effortless.

I have built a great relationship with the host of the show that has stood the test of time. She's become one of the hosts that I can confide in when it comes to making strategic decisions to make sweeping changes in the company, or just ask advice about an upcoming host.

It's another bonus of this job. I'm able to bounce ideas off and work with hosts of her caliber, and hopefully learn as much from them as they learn from me and my team.

It amazes me how she is capable of hosting 19 different shows, each show stemming from a different division of this software company, and completely disparate in their content, focus and nature. I don't normally "rate" shows on my own network, but she's a class act and really almost a force of nature. I'm going two thumbs up!

• • • • •

Get the up to date worksheets at www.jeffspenard.com and other tools for planning, producing and promoting your show. They're FREE, they just keep getting better with each new show and idea.

CHƎPTⲒR 9
BUILDING AND KEEPING YOUR AUDIENCE

Now that the "lights" are turned on and your show is up and running it's time to grow your audience and more importantly, turn them in to loyal fans.

There are a variety of free and low cost tools available for you to use to achieve this goal.

Email Marketing

Like everything in this world of s your database is truly the key to your success.

You need to build it not only from your radio or television website, but also from your/ social media and traditional websites. "Subscribe" is your operative word.

You have valuable information to share, how can you entice them to subscribe.

Maybe you create a PDF with 10 "tidbits" that will make their lives better. Or maybe it's a discount code for the purchase of your book or products. Maybe it's an invitation to your Online Training Seminar.

One way or the other you need to entice them to give over their data to you!

If you listen to terrestrial radio or watch TV you can get a good idea of how to attract and retain your audience. Simple words like FREE or EXCLUSIVE will generate more subscribers than just having a "sign up form".

Don't ask for too much data, maybe just their name and email address. Or maybe just their email address. The faster and easier it is to subscribe the larger your list will become.

Here's how to work the top four email "Software as a Service" companies. They are each unique and they all have a "free trial".

Check them out they can make your life easier in a variety of ways including avoiding the CAN SPAM Act while maintaining a healthy email database.

While you are building your subscriber base it's important to consider your strategy. How often do you hit the database? Is it weekly for your show? Do you use that database more often to sell your products and services?

Do you accept advertising on your blasts? Can you leverage the existing lists of your guests?

CONSTANT CONTACT

Constant Contact (www.constantcontact.com) is to some the gold standard of email marketing platforms. They have a variety of applications and an open API that allows developers to build integrations into your ecommerce, WordPress or other front end applications. They also have a wide variety of archived and ongoing marketing training seminars that might prove helpful not just for email marketing, but also for social media and other forms of online advertising.

They bill based upon the number of contacts you have in your database, not on the number of emails you send per month. This is cost effective if you send a lot of emails to the same list, like a weekly newsletter, or an email highlighting this week's guest or topic.

SEND GRID

Send Grid (www.sendgrid.com) has less features than Constant Contact but does offer good value for the money. Maybe not as much as Send in Blue below, but does have some interesting features if you're looking to send up to 100,000 emails per month. They have an easy to use drag and drop email creator, open APIs and some nice reporting features. They also offer A/B split testing in order for you to test which layout, content, message, etc. work best for your listeners or clients.

They also offer up to 12,000 emails per month for free at a limit of 400 emails per day.

SENDINBLUE

Send in Blue (www.sendinblue) is a relative newcomer to the email game. While not quite as feature rich as Constant Contact in terms of emails, they do offer SMS (Short Messaging Service) otherwise known as text messaging. They also have an open API, form creator and a variety of plugins for popular CMS systems like WordPress, PrestaShop and Magento among others.

They also offer 9,000 free emails per month (albeit at 300 emails per day) if you'd like to try it out. Send In Blue's pricing is the most cost effective starting at $7.97 per month for 40,000 emails, not based upon the number of subscribers you have. They also have a Pay as You Go Plan where the credits you purchase never expire.

ENGAGE

There is an old saying in broadcasting, "Fake it till you Make it". This is a good saying when you are starting a new show. Even if your content is good, you might want to consider using some other tactics to encourage your listeners to engage with the show, your website and your newsletter list.

If you have a book or a 10 page PDF that you can use to entice them to subscribe, even better. Or maybe a "free" consultation.

Consider the "value" of each subscriber. Are they worth $50, $100, or $5? Subscribers not only help increase your listener base using "share" and social media features, but they also provide other opportunities to create revenue for your business or organization.

LISTEN

It's a good idea to periodically listen to the top shows in your genre to see what innovative ideas they might be using to increase and maintain their audience. Another good source of ideas is to listen to some of the top "marketing" shows. Why not listen to the pros and see how they are deploying new tactics to increase and maintain your listeners.

· · · · ·

Get the up to date worksheets at www.jeffspenard.com and other tools for planning, producing and promoting your show. They're FREE, they just keep getting better with each new show and idea.

CHAPTER 10
USING PRESS RELEASES TO PROMOTE YOUR BROADCAST

Press releases are a good way to promote your show. There is a great debate about the search engine value of press releases and how to do them.

The most important part of your press release is content, it needs to be succinct and contain valuable, unique information.

Press Release Guidelines

Under standard distribution it will take two business days at minimum from the day we receive the release. We recommend releasing the news item the day before the show for maximum effectiveness.

- Your guest should be widely known to the general public. This usually means celebrities, well-known authors, or political figures. If the guest is only known to certain people or in a limited field, this may not get a wide distribution on the search engines.

- If the show is about a topic it needs to relate to something that is news-related and immediately current.

- The press release should be 50% related to the guest or topic, 40% related to the show and the network, and 10% or less related to any other interests, events or promotions.

- The press release needs to be almost entirely pertaining to or tied in to your radio show and nothing else. It is designed to drive traffic to our network and your show in particular.

Press Release Template – please follow this format:

Headline Announces News in Title Case, Ideally Under 100 Characters

The summary paragraph is a little longer synopsis of the news, elaborating on the news in the headline in one to four sentences. The summary uses sentence case, with standard capitalization and punctuation.

City, State (Press Release Service) Month 1, 2015 -- The lead sentence contains the most important information in 25 words or less. Grab your reader's attention here by simply stating the news you have to announce. Do not assume that your reader has read your headline or summary paragraph; the lead should stand on its own. Be sure to include your important keywords in the headline, summary and lead paragraph. Add your Web address here for a quick link and to reinforce your site name and location.

A news release, like a news story, keeps sentences and paragraphs short, about three or four lines per paragraph. The first couple of paragraphs should answer the who, what, when, where, why and how questions. The news media may take information from a news release to craft a news or feature article or may use information in the release word-for-word.

The standard press release is 300 to 800 words and written in a word processing program that checks spelling and grammar before submission.

The ideal headline is 80 characters long. Most press release sites will accept headlines with a maximum of 170 characters. We recommend writing your headline and summary last, to be sure you include the most important news elements in the body of the release. Use title case in the headline only, capitalizing every word except for prepositions and articles of three characters or less.

The rest of the news release expounds on the information provided in the lead paragraph. It includes quotes from key staff, customers or subject matter experts. It contains more details about the news you have to tell, which can be about something unique or controversial or about a prominent person, place or thing. It also includes links to your Web site in this form: http://www.mywebsite.com .

Typical topics for a news release include announcements of new products or of a strategic partnership, the receipt of an award, the publishing of a book, the release of new software or the launch of a new Web site. The tone is neutral and objective, not full of hype or text that is typically found in an advertisement. Avoid directly addressing the consumer or your target audience. The use of "I," "we" and "you" outside of a direct quotation is a flag that your copy is an advertisement rather than a news release.

Do not include an e-mail address in the body of the release. If you do, it will be protected from spam bots with a notice to that effect, which will overwrite your e-mail address.

"The final paragraph of a traditional news release contains the least newsworthy material," said Mario Bonilla, member services director for Super Widget Company. "But for an online release, it's typical to restate and summarize the key points with a paragraph like the next one."

For additional information on the news that is the subject of this release (or for a sample, copy or demo), contact Mary Smith or visit http://www.mywebsite.com. You can also include details on product availability, trademark acknowledgment, etc. here.

About XYZ Company:

Include a short corporate backgrounder, or "boilerplate," about the company or the person who is newsworthy before you list the contact person's name and phone number.

A Sample Press Release from our Radio Department appears below.

Straight Up with Chris: Real Talk on Business and Parenthood Celebrates 2 Year Broadcast Anniversary on VoiceAmerica's Variety Channel

Straight Up with Chris: Real Talk on Business and Parenthood, the innovative and educational interactive parenting talk radio show hosted by entrepreneur and author – Chris Efessiou surpasses two year broadcast anniversary and begins its third year of broadcasting on VoiceAmerica Talk Radio.

PHOENIX – Bringing guests such as author of the best-selling The One Minute Manager Dr. Ken Blanchard, award winning author and internationally recognized expert on children Michele Borba, Ed.D, and Dennis Hastert, Former Speaker of the U. S. House of Representatives. Efessiou has built a loyal listenership and continues to inform, entertain and educate listeners worldwide.

"Chris Efessiou brings to the table exactly the type of inspirational, educational and engaging talk radio show that our listeners are searching out," stated Jeff Spenard, CEO of VoiceAmerica. "He brings leaders from both the business world and experts on parenting together combined with his personal experience of being a single father to help guide and invigorate parents from all walks of life."

Straight Up with Chris is broadcast live every Thursday at 3 PM Pacific Time on the VoiceAmerica Variety Channel. Archives of Straight Up with Chris can be found at http://www.voiceamerica.com/show/2065/straight-up-with-chris-real-talk-on-business-and-parenthood

"I am so pleased that Chris Efessiou has been with us for three years. He is a pleasure to work with and his show is truly inspirational to so many global listeners each week. He has truly affected change in both the parenting and leadership world, guiding them through many areas in life," stated Tacy Trump, Senior Executive Producer.

Chris Efessiou is the Founder and Chief Development Officer of Chris Efessiou & Team Companies offering workshops, speaking engagements, consulting, coaching and media. He focuses on educating, motivating and inspiring people on how to transfer their business skills to their personal relationships. Chief topic areas include Leadership Development, the Art of Negotiation, Mentorship, Communications, Risk Assessment and Management.. For information please visit http://www.ChrisEfessiou.com.

The VoiceAmerica TM Network offers the latest conversations in a talk radio format, providing education, interaction, and advice on key issues live, on demand as well as through podcast download. If interested in hosting a talk show on VoiceAmerica Network, contact Jeff Spenard, President of Internet Radio at 480-294-6417 or at jeff.spenard@voiceamerica.com

Contact Executive Producer:

_____ at (480) _____
for advertising / sponsorship or other show details.

About Straight Up with Chris: Real Talk on Business and Parenthood

Straight Up with Chris: Real Talk on Business and Parenthood is a light-hearted show discussing serious issues aimed to encourage, inspire, teach and support parents in applying their business skills to the business of parenting and personal relationships. Chris, along with his guests, will share unique principles, how-tos, ideas, methods, expertise, humor and personal experiences to best serve the needs of the listeners. Listeners have an opportunity to suggest topics for discussion and as a result our show will always be relevant to you.

Listeners can download the current versions of the VoiceAmerica Talk Radio App at:

Google Play: https://play.google.com/store/apps/details?id=com.airkast.VA_MASTER&hl=en

iTunes: https://itunes.apple.com/us/app/voiceamerica-talk-radio-network/id412135954?mt=8#

Kindle: http://www.amazon.com/AirKast-Inc-Voice-America/dp/B00IGH8WPO

About VoiceAmerica/World Talk Radio LLC

World Talk Radio, LLC is the world leader in online media broadcasting and the largest producer and distributor of live internet based talk radio and TV, delivering over 1,000 hours of programming weekly on its VoiceAmerica™ Network (http://www.voiceamerica.com) as well as live and on-demand video content on VoiceAmerica.TV (http://www.voiceamerica.tv). Featuring more than 200 hosts broadcasting to seven niche community based channels: its flagship VoiceAmerica™ Variety Channel, VoiceAmerica™, Empowerment, VoiceAmerica™ Health & Wellness Channel, VoiceAmerica™ Business Channel, VoiceAmerica Sports, 7th Wave Channel, and VoiceAmerica™ Kids Channel. VoiceAmerica™ TV offers targeted and exclusive video programming channels. VoiceAmerica™ /World Talk Radio, LLC is one of the pioneers in internet broadcasting, producing and syndicating online audio and video, offering an innovative, effective and comprehensive digital broadcast platform. Digital Publishing through its 14 years of broadcast and media experience along with our seasoned staff of Executive Producers, Production and Host Services Group, VoiceAmerica™ /World Talk Radio, LLC provides an internet radio and video platform for new, emerging and veteran media personalities to expand and monetize their business and brand in an online digital medium.

Listeners can download the current versions of the VoiceAmerica Talk Radio App at:

Google Play: https://play.google.com/store/apps/ details?id=com.airkast.VA_MASTER&hl=en

iTunes: https://itunes.apple.com/us/app/ voiceamerica-talk-radio-network/id412135954?mt=8#

Kindle: http://www.amazon.com/ AirKast-Inc-Voice-America/dp/B00IGH8WPO

· · · · ·

Get the up to date worksheets at www.jeffspenard.com and other tools for planning, producing and promoting your show. They're FREE, they just keep getting better with each new show and idea.

CHƎPTER II
SELF SYNDICATING YOUR BROADCAST

So you have a couple of shows in the can so to speak. Now you're looking to expand your audience without having to spend a lot, or any money.

Ready for your evil secret plan!

If you set it up with a broadcast network, or are crafty enough to create your own feed you're going to want to be in places that people can find you, and not just on the web, mobile baby, so they can listen to you live or on demand wherever they are at the time.

Here are that mandatory places to be if you're going to self-syndicate. BTW – if you're playing with a broadcasting company like mine, this should be automatic, but if you're doing if yourself here's the scoop.

1. TuneIn

TuneIn.com is essentially a radio aggregator. According to their website they have 100,00+ "stations" and over 50 million listeners per month. It's not difficult to add your show to their directory, but you will need an XML or RSS (Real Simple Syndication) feed so that when new shows are added they automatically appear on TuneIn. You will need one of these types of feeds for pretty much everything going forward, so make sure your broadcasting partner or platform creates these for you. They accept MP3 and

According to the TuneIn website, here's what you need to do:

You can add a podcast by emailing broadcaster-support@tunein.com with the following:

1) Title
2) Location
3) Logo (png/jpg) 1200x1200 and less than 2 mbs
4) XML/RSS Feed URL
5) Website address
6) Genre
7) Email
8) Twitter (optional)

** If you are using blogtalkradio/spreaker, note that future episode information listed in your feed that does not include the audio associated with them may corrupt the feed on TuneIn. We recommend only adding new episode information to your feed when the audio is available to prevent this.

2. Sticher

www.sticher.com is similar to TuneIn with 40,000+ radio stations and podcasts. Signing up is just as easy using an RSS feed and a form that you can find here https://www.stitcher.com/content-faq. Sticher has a mobile app and some other nice tools for broadcasters. Again, check with your broadcasting platform, this might already have happened and you don't need to bother with it.

3. iTunes

Apple's iconic iTunes also provides access to new listeners by submitting your podcast to their iTunes player directory. Here you will need a RSS feed. You can find out how to submit a podcast to iTunes here https://buy. itunes.apple.com/WebObjects/MZFinance.woa/wa/ publishPodcast .

You will need a free Apple ID in order to submit, essentially like registering for iTunes to download the player in the first place.

4. PodcastDirectory.com

   One of the original podcasting resources and still very well placed on the search engines. Submission is free and the form is really simple. Remember, like any other form you are filling out for marketing purposes, complete all of the fields in the form.

5. iPodder.org

   A fairly robust directory of podcasts. Sign up is free. Here's where you sign up http://www.ipodder.org/hints/new. Requires an XML file.

6. Embeddable Players

   An embeddable player is simply a piece of code, usually either an iFrame or JavaScript that enables you to "add" your content to almost any website. Most embeddable players allow you to size on the fly the size of the media you wish to display.

   One of the benefits that leading internet talk radio broadcasting platforms provide is an embeddable player, the same is true for internet television. An embeddable player is what you see when someone has a YouTube video on their website or blog that isn't just a link. These are handy for your own use and audience growth and maintenance.

7. Here's where you could place that player (or a link if it's just one show).

    1) Your website

    2) Your blog

    3) Other people's websites that are interested in the same topicality

    4) Your Guest's website

    5) Your advertisers and sponsors websites

    6) Membership Groups – a trade association specializing in some vertical industry, a political party or social issue organization, a professional organization would be some high traffic sites that can build and HOLD audience. These organization and there large existing traffic with frequently returning visitors provide you with a nice piggybacking opportunity.

        Consider offering them advertising on your show for free or a discounted rate or a Guest spot on your show.

8. FROM YOUR OWN WEBSITE

Depending upon what platform, such as Joomla or WordPress creating an RSS feed from your "podcast" category is pretty much built into the site as a basic function. There are a series of plugins or extensions for free that can provide additional functionality and ease of use.

If your site doesn't automatically create feeds, you could also create other sorts of feeds or embeddable players for a monthly fee at http://www.rapidfeeds.com/ . Try their "FREE TRIAL" and test it out to see if it does what you want.

If you're broadcasting on a professional platform these are automatically generated for you. Another benefit of going pro.

. . . . .

Get the up to date worksheets at www.jeffspenard.com and other tools for planning, producing and promoting your show. They're FREE, they just keep getting better with each new show and idea.

CHAPTER 12
USING SOCIAL MEDIA TO PROMOTE YOUR BROADCAST

Social media this and social media that. Twitter, Facebook, Instagram, Reddit, LinkedIN. How much communication can we really have! It will explode your mind.

Social media is this era's Telephone. Except that everyone is listening to your conversation!

This is a good and a bad thing at the same time. So before we get into the strategic part of Social Media, let's set some guidelines.

Social Media Guidelines

These are the basic guidelines for social media use on behalf of your show, yourself and your endeavors.

Live your own public image philosophy. In online social networks, the lines between public and private, personal and professional are blurred. Just by identifying yourself you are creating perceptions about your expertise. Be sure that all content associated with you is consistent with your work and your philosophy (that social media is about building relationships – not a numbers game).

⏰ OPTIMUM TIMING FOR SOCIAL POSTS

	BEST	WORST
FACEBOOK	1PM - 4PM	8PM - 8AM
TWITTER	1PM - 3PM	8PM - 9AM
PINTEREST	2PM - 4PM	5PM - 7PM
	8PM - 1AM	
GOOGLE+	9AM - 11AM	6PM - 8AM
LINKEDIN	7AM - 9AM	10PM - 6AM
	5PM - 6PM	

- **Understand privacy settings on outposts.** Don't expect all of your social media use to be work-related, but do expect that it's a good idea you to keep the items you share with your close personal friends separate from what you share with your work "friends" and audience. We will discuss this below.

- **Be yourself.** Never impersonate someone else, or purposely obscure your identity. Build your own reputation. Care about what you are talking about. Add to the conversation.

- **State when it's your personal opinion versus the show or a guest's opinion.** This is most important when you have a co-host or are hosting the show on behalf of a company or product, especially if part of your job is hosting the show!

- **Write what you know.** Stick to your area of expertise and provide unique, individual perspectives on what's going on at your show and in the world.

- **Don't tell secrets.** Respect proprietary information and content, and confidentiality. Don't discuss client work without permission or post phone numbers or emails. Web addresses or a link to the show page or episode will suffice.

- **Don't spam. Ever.** You can link to other your show blog posts or information about services but do it subtly and only in response to a specific query.

- **Give credit where credit is due.** Always attribute when quoting someone else. Make sure images are shareable through Creative Commons, and attribute them, too. Never use copyrighted material without permission.

- **Mistakes happen.** Let the team help you fix your mistakes. Most of the time, admitting your mistake and moving on is enough. When it isn't, the team can come together to find a solution to any problem.

- **Share the love.** We believe in sharing and linking to the best content from all over the web. A link is not an endorsement, so don't be shy about sharing something from a "competitor" if you feel it is worthwhile to our clients and friends.

- **Be a good conversationalist.** Monitor and reply to comments in a timely manner, when a response is appropriate; pause and wait if you are having an emotional response to something – or show someone else first before you hit the publish button.

- **Be clear, but not defensive.** Be polite and professional, especially when you disagree with someone. If you find yourself working too hard to defend, take a step back, let the community defend for you (because they will).

- **Remember everything online is discoverable.** If you can't show it to your mother or a judge, don't post it. If in doubt, ask.

- **Always be learning.** This space is fast-moving and ever-evolving. Read more than you write. Ask questions. Link to others and always build relationships. That's what our work is all about.

- **FOLLOW THE 80/20 Rule**: This goes for all of the social media sites. 80% of your posts should be "social" – meaning they are interesting and relevant to your audience or topic, but not necessarily promoting your specific products or services. This Rule helps to position you as a "news destination" and reliable information source for your audience and followers, while not overwhelming them with your sales pitch.

- **If you mention a guests website, an event, a news story or pretty much anything else you can link to on your show, make sure you tell the audience they can find out more by going to your Facebook page, or Twitter account.** This will help engage your listening audience on social media, while endearing your to your guests. Always make sure to include a brief introduction to the link versus just including the link.

Best Times to Post to Social Media

Post when the audience is listening, not just when "business" is open. This will ensure more user engagement. According to Fast Company (http://www.fastcompany.com/3036184/how-to-be-a-success-at-everything/the-best-and-worst-times-to-post-on-social-media-infograph) here are the best (and sometimes worst) times to post to your social media accounts.

FACEBOOK

The best time to post to Facebook is 1-4 PM during the week, peaking at around 3 PM. The lowest points are on the weekends before 8 AM and after 8 PM. One of the reasons for the afternoon "best time" is that during the work week, after lunch most people who cannot avail themselves of a quick nap, need a little motivation and mind clearing in the middle of their "food coma". A quick engagement on Facebook, whether that is to just a take a little break, check on the competition or make plans for the evening provide that little break. Although this probably isn't the best office policy for employees, it's more than likely going to happen anyway.

TWITTER

The best time to post to Twitter is just before lunchtime. Studies have shown that most people check and engage their

Twitter accounts during lunch using their mobile devices. You can increase your retweets by up to 48% by including an image. Remember the rule of thumb for all images (or as many as possible) that you post across social media – include your @yourname as a bare minimum, and preferably your web address as well. This will help to increase your followers regardless of where the image might end up. For example: your post an image with a quote of the day to Twitter, it is very possible that the image ends up on someone else's Facebook, Instagram, Pinterest or Tumbler account, even though it originated on your Twitter account.

LINKEDIN

As most people use LinkedIn primarily for business purposes the best time to post is Tuesday through Thursday during business hours. Once you get to Friday after lunch people begin to check out mentally, and weekends are virtually a dead zone on Saturday and Sunday. However, pay attention to the LinkedIN groups that you have joined and monitor them and engage there versus posting directly to your personal or corporate LinkedIn page. Monday's aren't the best day for LinkedIn either as busy executives or company owners are often catching up after the weekend, dealing with employee issues, having sales or management meetings and simply going through the mass of information they received over the weekend via electronic and snail mail and just don't have time for social media.

PINTEREST

Pinterest is a bit of a different animal in terms of audience. Pinterest is almost more of a "shopping" site – whether the follower is searching for recipes, or "ideas" for projects or fashion or almost anything that lends itself more to visual imagery than reading. Pinterest user interest is highest in the evenings and on weekends and lowest during weekday business hours.

TUMBLR

Tumble, similar to Pinterest, is a bit of a different animal. Tumblr is quite useful for entertainment seekers and followers of celebrities and has a bit of a younger audience than other social media networks. Tumblr might not be the best use of your time if your show is business oriented compared to LinkedIn. However, if you show is entertainment, hobby or sports related, it could prove very useful in reaching a specific audience, and it's very easy to use. The best time to post to Tumblr is "after hours" when people are winding down and looking for less heady information such as entertainment news or interviews.

GOOGLE+

Interestingly enough, Google+ users tend to check and engage first thing in the morning. One reason for this is that Google has the largest community of integrated tools users, i.e. Gmail, Google Voice, Google News, Google Analytics, Google Ads, etc. So the logic behind posting early to Google+

is that Google users tend to check email, news, etc. first thing to get their day started and have a "routine" they follow when accessing Google services.

INSTAGRAM

To a certain extent the jury is still out on the best times to post to Instagram. As the name suggests, it's instant. Instagram is best suited for promoting yourself via pictures versus written content. For example, you're attending an industry event where you might meet an industry leader, a celebrity or even just someone you'd like to do business with. This is where the "selfie" comes in to play. Because these sort of events don't always happen during business hours, and it's "instant" you'll want to post these photos pretty much immediately without being rude to the "real person" you've just engaged!

Best Practices for Facebook Posts

1. **Keep things positive**Being positive breeds engagement and encourages sharing.

2. **Provide information**

   The most appealing updates are ones that offer something, but don't disclose everything — this increases the likelihood that fans will click.

3. **Provide a link**

   If you're going to provide a link, use a Google URL Shortener (http://goo.gl/), or another link-shortening service so you can track how many people are clicking through. Even if we're all posting the same link on different accounts, by using a Google URL Shortener we can track the effectiveness of each individual action.

4. **Include images**

   Posts with images get the highest amount of engagement on Facebook, so be sure to include one when you can. The perfect size is 800×600.

5. **Make your posts mobile-friendly**

   Use simple imagery that can be easily seen on mobile devices — 70% of your fans read your posts on their phone.

6. **Engage with users**

   Posts aren't the only activities that grab attention — comments and responses do, too. Engage with people and build relationships through conversation.

7. **Be available**

   You will want to maximize your engagement by being available to your audience to respond to their comments, especially if you've asked a question. This doesn't mean that you should simply ignore the rest of your life and site and constantly hit refresh waiting for comments, but you should check in several times per day, or use one of the tools highlighted in this chapter to manage not just your Facebook account, but your other social media accounts as well.

8. **Use Hashtags**

   Facebook now allows Hashtags to identify the topic of what you are posting about. Using Hashtags in your Facebook posts helps people find your posts (see HASHTAGS below).

Best Practices for Twitter Posts

1. **Call to action**

   Give a clear call to action so your readers know what you want them to do.

2. **Punctuation**

Don't sacrifice grammar because you only have 140 characters.

3. **Format**

Use questions, facts, and figures to engage your audience and drive retweets.

4. **Mentions**

Use @ mentions to prompt influencers to engage with you and make sure you respond. i.e. @yourshow or @ yourshowname etc.

5. **Retweet**

Retweet relevant content for your audience. Don't forget to leave 20 characters so people can add content or comments.

Here is a great article on Retweeting http://www. hashtags.org/platforms/twitter/what-is-a-retweet/

In addition, there are several Retweet Commands that can enhance how those Retweets are shared, handled, attributed, etc. Here are the links for a full list of commands.

FROM YOUR MOBILE: https://support.twitter.com/ articles/14020-twitter-sms-commands

Here is a great article on Retweeting Etiquette
http://www.hashtags.org/how-to/etiquette-how-to/
twitter-etiquette-retweeting-the-right-way/

Best Practices for Pinterest Posts

1. **No human faces**
   Images with no human faces are shared 23% more than those with them.

2. **Multiple colors**
   Images with dominant colors — red, dark green, pink — are shared 3x more than images that don't contain them.

3. **Light and color**
   Images with 50% color saturation are repinned 4x more often than those with 100%, and 10x more than black and white images.

4. **Minimal background**
   Use a compelling background that doesn't take up more than 40% of your image, otherwise your repins will decrease by 50%.

5. **Use red**
   Red or orange images are repinned twice as often

6. **Portrait style**

   Vertically oriented images perform better than those that are horizontally oriented; the perfect ratios are 2:3 and 4:5.

7. **Top Tips for Brands using Instagram:**

   Understand your brand's audience, even in Instagram. Amex or Burberry followers will expect something different than Starbucks, Red Bull or MTV's.

   Create a theme for your content and be consistent. Constant product placement is not a theme.

   Take lots of photographs and make them aesthetically pleasing and creative.

   Give your followers a reason to want to follow your brand in Instagram.

8. Spread out posts like you would any other network. Post once or twice a day.

9. Engage with your followers. Comment. Follow back. Like things. Be human.

10. Tell an interesting brand story through your images and captions.

11. Lastly, throw a creative #hashtag contest or #project to get interaction going and amplify it across your already-established social networks. Point to your now-built-up Instagram account and get followers involved. And, if you must roll-out a product photo, give it a human touch by making it creative, funny or awesome. Treat Instagram like your brand's lifestyle magazine.

Best Practices for Google+ Posts

1. Use hashtags

Increase your page's reach by adding relevant hashtags. Google+ automatically adds hashtags for key/trending topics.

2. Tag brands and people

When brands and people are tagged, they receive notifications from Google+ — this can lead them to engage with your post.

3. Trending topics

Get involved with the "hot topics" to improve visibility and show that your brand is keeping pace with real-time events.

4. Use images

Use full-sized images — 800×600 — to make your posts stand out. Tiny images and thumbnails pale in comparison.

5. **Find communities**

   Find relevant communities and contribute your expertise — your engagement will increase as a result.

Tools to Help Manage Your Social Media

Managing your social media campaign across a variety of networks can be daunting, but it doesn't have to be. There are a variety of free and paid tools that you can use to help schedule your posts, manage your comments and user engagement and analyze the effectiveness of your message. Here are just a few that I can recommend. As social media continues to grow and expand exponentially more of these tools will come online. Most have a free package and a paid package, usually not terribly expensive. Keep in mind that the "free" package most likely will not have all of the features you might want, and will probably limit you to a finite number of social media sites, usually Facebook and Twitter.

Scheduling your posts is one of the most important features of these tools. Scheduling allows you to plan out a week, or even a month at a time at one sitting, while allowing you to interject new posts as you require.

For example, you have your guests or topics planned and booked for a month in advance. Rather than have to remember every week to post to your social media accounts you can promote the upcoming show days in advance, the day of the show and after the show have aired (if you have archived versions of your show available), you can do this all at one sitting and as Ron Popeil is famous for saying about his rotisserie cooking devices, "Set it and forget it".

HOOTSUITE

HootSuite is one of the longest standing Social Media tools on the market. They offer both free and paid packages ranging from individual to Enterprise. You can view the plans here https://hootsuite.com/plans.

Depending upon your plan (the free one allows 3 social networks) HootSuite can connect you with over 35 social media sites that you can manage with one login.

HootSuite also has over 120 "snap on" apps to enhance your effectiveness. Some of these apps require a one time fee, some are monthly fees and some are free. These apps range from enhanced posting capabilities, to engagement monitoring to integration with third party marketing applications such as Marketo.

HootSuite also affords a high level of monitoring and security as well. With their Pro and Enterprise packages you can have multiple team members working on your social media accounts at the same time, which is nice if you have a staff!

HootSuite, like most of the social media management tools, has a free trial period and costs range from free to $9.99 per mont for the Pro Package (best value) to custom Enterprise packages.

They also have an extensive learning and resource library along with ongoing free training as social media continues to expand and mature.

CAPZOOL

Capzool is a relatively new player on the social media side, and a little pricier than HootSuite at $49 per month, but they do have some interesting integrated features like press releases, contact management, press release and deal publishing tools, slide creation, SMS (text messaging) capabilities, reputation management tools and a lot more.

Capzool does have a free option, but it's highly limited. They also have a free trial that might be worth checking out, especially if you require the "non social" tool set that they have. You can check out their plans here http://capzool.com/pricing.

SPROUT SOCIAL

Sprout Social has been around for quite awhile and offer a complete integrated suite of social media management tools. The downside here is the $59 per user per month pricing structure on the Deluxe Plan (the lowest level). You can check out their pricing here http://sproutsocial.com/pricing.

Sprout Social is best suited for larger teams and more sophisticated integrations like Zen Desk help desk or the Salesforce sales platform.

They do have a 30 day free trial that doesn't require a credit card enabling you to check it out.

BUFFER

Think of Buffer as a powerful scheduling tool replete with RSS integration for automatic posting and a small set of tools. HootSuite does all of these functions as well, but Buffer can also be a useful tool in conjunction with your primary social media management tools to "spread out" where your posts are coming from for the purposes of search engine optimization and reputation management.

IFTTT

IF THIS THEN THAT is a "recipe creation tool" amongst other things. With a simple drag and drop interface you can create rules that help automate and cross promote your content. For example, you have a blog and you want your blog posts to automatically post to Facebook, you simply drag and drop your IF THIS THEN THAT "recipe" and viola.

IFTTT also works very well in conjunction with HootSuite and Buffer. IFTTT is FREE and comes as an iOS or Android app allowing you to set up your recipes and control them from anywhere you are. Check them out here https://ifttt.com/products.

Understanding Hashtags

So what exactly is a hashtag?

The simplified definition is: hashtags are like keywords which can be used to organize messages on a social network. This then facilitates the searching and grouping of messages with given hashtags. Hashtags are preceded by the pound sign (#) and can be a word or a short phrase (i.e. #Hashtag or #ThisIsAHashtag)

More technical definitions can be found on Wikipedia and Wiktionary.

Who defines hashtags?

You do. You can place a pound (#) sign in front of any keyword(s) in your message and turn them into hashtags. However, the power of hashtags comes from other people using the same keyword(s) so that by clicking on a hashtag you can get a group of other messages on that topic.

How can I use hashtags?

Typical uses of hashtags:

- Express emotions: #surprised #speechless #frustrated
- Identify places or brands or events: #Hawaii #Ferrari #CoolEvent
- Make recommendations: #MustRead #MustWatch #NowPlaying
- Connect with like-minded individuals: #CatLovers #TVaddicts

Hashtags should make your messages easier to organize and find. The trick is to hashtag keywords that other people would use when looking for the content contained in your message. You can do a quick search for keywords prior to posting your message to see which hashtags are popular (called "trending").

Three common mistakes to avoid:

1. Hashtagging every word (i.e. #I #am #so #excited #today)

2. Hashtagging the same word more than once (i.e. It is my #birthday. Here is a photo of my #birthday cake, my #birthday presents, and my awesome #birthday party!)

3. Separating keywords. If your keyword is "black cat" your hashtag should be #BlackCat. If you write it as #Black #Cat this will give you two different keywords: "black" and "cat".

Where can I place hashtags?

You can use hashtags anywhere in your message – in the main body itself or as a postscript at the end. Here is an example with a hashtag in the main body of the message and two hashtags at the end.

Check out this #TalkRadio show: http://www.your show. com/show/1501/turning-hard-times-into-good-times (except you'd want to shorten it with Google Shortener first!) #Finance #GoldMiningStocks

Why should I use hashtags?

There are a variety of reasons to use hashtags:

1. Increase exposure
2. Organize content
3. Create buzz
4. Create trends
5. Consolidate your "followers"
6. Engage your "followers"

Some Thoughts About Content

It is important as a radio show host to speak in abstracts when it comes to numbers.

EXAMPLE: Two Reasons.

Never say that. Say something like "The reasoning behind this idea is….." or "There are several reasons….."

One of my friends recently told me a story about how his son got in trouble at school where he is in 5th grade

He's a good kid, honor student, athlete, already kissed a girl and an all around good kid.

So one day the little "take home" sheet says "Call Teacher", so my friend's ex calls the teacher and the teacher informs her that "Your son said out loud that 'All girls are slow' in the middle of Physical Education"

My friend explained to me, happily, that this was almost the first time he and his EX agreed on something.

They explained to the boy to never speak in absolutes. He should have said "Most girls don't really run that fast", or "Some girls can run really fast, but most boys are faster", or

"Wow, that girl is pretty fast, could all girls be that fast, let's start a fact finding investigation".

This is an important concept to understand, not just for social media, but for your show, what you write, and almost the way you think.

Pick your words carefully. If you do, those words will serve you well. If you don't, everybody has a copy of your mistake and it can go viral.

Social Media is about the conversation.

You can't really control a conversation. It's impossible because there are more people than just you involved.

On the bright side, you can manipulate the conversation to your advantage. Social Media is a perfect tool for conversational manipulation!

After years of working with the big names and the big players and learning from them, I've been able to help scores of people take their idea, message or products from obscurity to prevalence.

The technology is ever changing. But the principles will always be the same.

These would be the initial considerations.

1. What do you want to get everyone talking about?

2. Identify the proper hashtags. We're using "taxes" and "men stink" as examples here. This part is where I tell you it's as easy as using the SEARCH function on the social media site to determine the best hashtags!

   You can also find out what hashtags are "trending" at https://www.hashtags.org/ or http://top-hashtags.com/. These sites can help you identify the best hashtags to use to find new followers, fans and conversations to join.

   One thing that is important to remember, using hashtags in a creepy, spammy way to trick people into engaging with you is likely to backfire. For example, your show is about Human Resources, but Lindsay Lohan just did something to get herself on the news and is "trending", don't try to hijack the teeny bopper audience hoping that you will get some followers, you will probably just get negative comments.

   However, let's pretend your HR show topic of the week is "Finding a Better Job" and the hashtag "minimum wage" is trending, now you're in the proper ballpark.

3. JOIN topical groups and follow larger Twitter, LinkedIn, Google +, etc. groups and join their conversations and pay attention to the trending hashtags that they are using.

4. Make it short and simple – like "I don't want to pay these taxes @you #taxes" or "Men Stink! Anyone have dating tips for my new book? @you #menstink".

   You have now invaded other people's conversations, jumped right in!

5. Decide and plan what your answers are BEFORE the questions come. Believe it or not about half of your audience isn't tuning in to hear your point of view, but rather seeking validation for their own ideas. They might not actually call into the show because of fear or they are in the office or whatever reason, but they will engage on social media as it provides a false sense of anonymity and "security".

6. Encourage "shares" to increase the pass around value of your audience. Let's pretend you have a radio or tv show about Human Resources. You could create a "graphic series" highlighting your philosophy or stratagem that holds a small intrinsic value that is worth your audience sharing.

It doesn't necessarily have to be a statistically laden infographic, maybe it's a quote you found on Bartlett's or another online quote site. It is important to remember to always include your web address or at the very least your @yourshowname or @yourname on your graphic.

7. USING OTHER PEOPLE'S CONTENT TO GET WHAT YOU WANT. If you have a blog, write a blog post commenting on a news story or other piece of content. Use "quotation marks" around any copy that you reference, as well as ALWAYS include a link to the original source material. The benefit of this is that you rapidly have a topic to expound upon, and their expert opinions, or your being "on top of the news" adds to your credibility.

Other Sites To Consider

REDDIT

REDDIT is a volunteer administrator conversation driven community of "sub-communities" based upon topics, stories and commentary. You can start conversations, join conversations and users vote up or down the value of the content. REDDIT can backfire if you don't play by the rules, or it can generate a tremendous amount of traffic to your site if you play nice. The community is very protective of their "protocols". It's not right for every business model, but can prove very effective. Here's an excellent, detailed write up on best practices for Businesses on REDDIT http://www.business-2community.com/social-media/reddit-01123897.

MEETUP

Meetup is the world's largest community of local groups with more than 9,000 local groups using meetup to plan local meetings or events. If you have the time, and your business model affords you the opportunity to expand your reach locally on a face to face basis, Meetup can become an invaluable resource for you to quickly search for, join and essentially get invited to local, relative groups that are getting together. http://meetup.com.

FORUMS

Depending upon your industry and marketplace there may be a variety of influential "forums" speaking specifically to you topical interest and expertise. Do a Google search for "_____ forums" and see what you can find.

Most forums have specific guidelines regarding joining and posting. For example, in order to start a conversation or "thread" you must have posted at least 5 comments on other people's "threads". A thread is simply a conversation started by a member. For example, "Does anyone have a recommendation on the best small business accounting software?"

Often forums also have directories, job postings, special offers and other community based freebies you can take advantage of once you join.

Again, read the guidelines carefully to avoid getting bounced off, or irritating fellow members of the community.

CHAPTER 13
MONETIZING YOUR BROADCAST

Wouldn't it be great if we all just got paid the salary we desired just for talking for an hour a day, or an hour a week? That would be awesome!

I wanted to be the cool DJ in the morning that spun the Van Halen records, told you the weather and said something you would think about all day.

You used to be able to go down to the station and apply, but those days are over.

Two things happened.

1. **Consolidation of the Terrestrial Radio Spectrum**
   It used to be that Patsy Cline or Loretta Lynn could work their way across the South hitting every radio station, playing live and giving interviews to get their songs played, and ultimately get paid.

Not anymore. Most of the "terrestrial" radio stations – meaning those that have a tower, a designated FCC signal and usually a certain format – oldies, talk, classic rock, etc. have been consolidated into major media companies.

This makes syndication difficult across those networks without an existing audience, and even better a proven track record of at least breaking even with some advertisers, creative "selling" or sponsorships.

2. The Internet

The Internet changed everything in the broadcast arena. Not simply because of the global nature of the audience, but in the way that the "airwaves" are controlled by a small consortium of large corporations, regulated by governments.

Back in 1997 when SurfNet Media created BoomBoxRadio.com and began what has become a revolution music and talk radio delivery to the masses, we came to the realization that EVERYONE could have a voice. Free Speech had once again emerged and we need to share it with the world.

A voice not regulated by George Carlin's dirty words, or our hosts ability to speak about health issues previously deemed "unhealthy" by the networks or government.

We asked ourselves, "Why would it be bad if women with ovarian cancer could have an open conversation with experts about their 'lady parts'"?

When can't people talk about right or left wing politics, or relationships, or their hobbies, or social cause that would never get "airtime" on an advertising and corporate controlled network? So we started breaking ground with a new model. Not so new to traditional radio, but brand new to internet talk radio, everyone could have a voice.

Seems now, more than 15 years later, that everyone has a "podcast", but that doesn't translate into audience loyalty or realizing the true benefit of your voice or message.

With that being said, understanding how to monetize your show without the benefit of a large corporation and national sales force is important if you're going to be laying out some hard earned cash, and more importantly, your time.

Not everyone wants to host a radio show to make money, some simply want to get their message out there cost-effectively, archived for posterity and engage the audience.

But it never hurts to offset costs!

Selling Time

Ever heard of Snapple? No one did either until Howard Stern started talking about it.

Now, we can all agree that Howard is a pro from dover when it comes to making things seems natural in his pitch. But don't discount the fact that he continually introduced Snapple's new flavors in his discourse with Robin.

He didn't do it because he liked Snapple, although it is a tasty beverage, he did it because they paid him to do it.

You can do the same with your airtime. Doesn't matter if you're small and you can only get them to give you free stuff and $200.

This one is the super secret of self promotion.

REMEMBER YOU ARE
THE MOST IMPORTANT PERSON
IN BROADCASTING!

They don't have a radio show, you do!

Remember the Clock and then forget about it!

Every minute of your airtime is worth money So make use of it, either for cash or for exposure. By the way, if you do affiliate programs, here's where you can get some clicks!

"Welcome to the Alice in Wonderland show, I'm sitting here chasing rabbits and I can't tell you that the best place to get rabbits is at www.rabbits.com – that where I get mine, and I couldn't be happier with my rabbit from www.rabbits.com . Mine is fluffy, and I couldn't make a decision on the website, so I called 1-800-RABBITS and spoke with a rabbit consultant and, Janye, my personal rabbit consultant made sure that me and Fluffy connected, and more than that, Jayne help me figure out the stuff about Fluffy's diet, cage and how I could actually train Fluffy how to do my laundry."

TO THE POINT: read my rabbit statement and time it on a clock

Costs you less than a minute or two, but for the Rabbit Lady that's gold!

Now take it to a different level. The Show isn't "Sponsored by Rabbit Lady", but you've come to love the Fluffy Rabbit that you may or may not have, and you talk about it at the beginning of the show every episode.

Sounds dumb, but people will tune in just to hear about Fluffy!

Just like they tuned in to Howard in the early days to hear about the new Flavor of Snapple.

I know I did, Snapple has a new Peach flavor, where can I get it?

That's the easy $200 per show or quarter, now take it to a different level!

How much would they pay for a five minute segment where "they" talked, not about their product directly, but about "health" and then you Segway into "Joe, doesn't your product do that?"

Maybe you don't do it every show, maybe they are recurring "guests" for that five minutes. Maybe they get brought on for discussions with the competion (and then double bill!).

Maybe they just want a 30 second and a one time that they can use when you send them the MP3 and make sure their "webmaster" knows how to put it on the site, or you send it out as an email? For them, to their people – now you piggybacked on their audience and "listenership" and gained new listeners for your show.

Inline Ads

If you have a website or blog, and they're pretty easy to create these days, there are some "clickable" advertising revenue opportunities that you might want to take a look at and add to your site.

GOOGLE ADSENSE

Google AdSense is one of the leading and easiest to implement online and mobile advertising solutions for bloggers, WordPress hosted sites and websites in general.

Here's a link to their tour which isn't really all that informative. https://www.google.com/adsense/www/en_US/tour/

Google AdSense is free to sign up for, and easy to learn, understand and implement at the basic level. There are a lot of advanced features and Google is pretty good about explaining these advanced options. You could always Google "how to increase adsense earnings" you will have a plethora of up to date and useful information.

Adsense CPC (Cost Per Click)

Adsense CPC is essentially how much money you get paid when someone clicks on the ad on your site, or on their mobile phone or in your YouTube account.

Depending upon the topic of your site the ads which show up might vary a bit. The ads key off the actual content of the site, as well as the keywords, descriptions and titles of the pages.

When doing your keyword research make sure you use the Approximate CPC column.

Another important factor is the content that you are adding to your blog or website. It needs to be tailored to the keyword research and what your readers are searching for, either on your site, or on Google. The more **original** content you can add, and on a regular basis the better. Avoid using pre-published content unless you are commenting on that previously published content, i.e. a story in The Wall Street Journal.

Although your radio show is broadcast to a global audience, when crafting your AdSense Ads it's important to select English speaking countries, and more than likely the United States, or your country of origin. This will result in higher Cost Per Click versus say having clicks from India.

Also, a good rule of thumb is not to have more than 3 ads showing per page. Image ads always pay out better than text ads.

Here are the top performing AdSense categories in terms of Cost Per Click.

1. Domains – Blogs on Internet Domains Like Yahoo, Go Daddy etc. It pays highest CPC.
2. Gadgets – Tech Gadgets like Apple products
3. Google – Google Products
4. Microsoft – MS office
5. Banking
6. Automobile
7. Health
8. Real Estate
9. Home Loans
10. Jobs
11. Dating & Romance – It pays lowest CPC.

In Google AdSense there are a variety of tools that you can deploy to track and evaluate the performance of your ads.

Ad Review Center

In the Ad Review Center you can see which categories of ads are showing on your website and how much they are paying. Here you can block ads that are showing that are irrelevant to your audience. Say for example that your site and show are about Personal Finance, but ads are showing from the Dating Category, block the dating category. This will help increase your Cost Per Click, as well as refining the relevancy of the ads that are shown to your audience.

Competitive Ad Filter

Similar to the Ad Review center in terms of blocking irrelevant ads. The Competitive Ad Filter allows you to block specific or general ads from appearing, as well as ads that might be showing from your competitors.

BING AND YAHOO ADS

Another solution for inline advertising is the Media.net solution http://www.media.net/. Their network of publishers is quite large and includes Bing and Yahoo!.

The tools and approach are nearly identical to AdSense with a few minor differences in terminology.

Traditional Ads

In concert with your "radio ads" you might consider packaging traditional online banner ads into your Media Kit

MAILING LISTS

To often we are worried about money. It freaks people out when you say "I'll give it away". Give it away. Not the advertising, but the show. We'll talk about that in Chapter 11.

In the advertising world you might call it "pass around value".

Like the copy of the newspaper in the Doctor's office. Even Gannett and every major newspaper counts "pass around value".

It's important to understand that your show ISN'T one off advertising for your sponsors. It lives forever, past the original broadcast, past the archive, past the download, but it lives on with the "share".

Unlike newspaper sales or even BS terrestrial or TV broadcast numbers from Nielsen, your show, and their advertising lives forever!

Don't be afraid of telling them that. It's a different form of advertising or sponsorship than some silly X games deal!

· · · · ·

Get the up to date worksheets at www.jeffspenard.com and other tools for planning, producing and promoting your show. They're FREE, they just keep getting better with each new show and idea.

EPILOGUE

So that's how you do it, or at least how I would do it! It changes so quickly in terms of technology that you can get lost and stray away from the value of content and the personal desire to share your information.

The ability to bring your message of hope, conspiracy or simply support a product or service is becoming increasingly available, and invaluable.

I hope that this book has provided some insight for you in the PLANNING of your radio or television project.

I've been encouraged through the process of sharing my experiences and expertise with you. I remembered what I love about broadcasting!

We're actually all born listeners, but someone has to talk! We all have a voice. We want the information. We want the interaction. We want to be entertained and we want it 24/7 and on demand.

Broadcasting has changed for the better by creating something that has the ability to last forever. We can all achieve a certain level of immortality by creating something that will probably last forever.

Don't be scared of the microphone or the camera. Plan ahead. Ask a Professional. Set Goals.

This book is the beginning, please go to www.jeffspenard.com and sign up for the newsletter and for updates. It won't just be me, I'm bringing in the most talented people in internet marketing to help us all continue the new media revolution that's 20 years into the making.

Thank you for buying this book. I hope that it will help you. Please don't hesitate to contact me if I can't help you achieve your broadcast goals. Feel free to email me direct at jeff@jeffspenard.com with your ideas.

More Books From

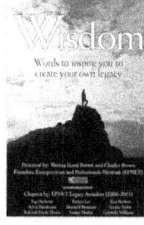

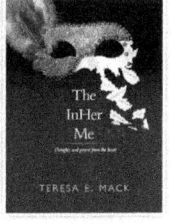

PERFECT PUBLISHING

UMBRELLA MARKETING
Amplify Your Message!
KEN ROCHON, JR.

BECOMING THE PERFECT NETWORKER

The Centurion World Traveller Game
Ken Rochon, Jr.

The Absolute Spin...
Make Retries the Moment!
Ken Rochon. Jr.

LESSONS OF REDEMPTION
#DoRight
A MEMOIR BY KEVIN SHIRD

THE PERFECT NETWORK-OUT
BALANCING, CREATING & LIVING WEALTH + WELLNESS
KEN ROCHON

CHICKEN POOP for the SOLE

Wisdom
Words to inspire you to create your own legacy

So...I Got Fired From THAT Job!
BRISCOE

Don't Waste My Career
GAYELA BYNUM

Empowerment Beyond
A 6-week self study yoga program practicing reflection, wisdom and peace
SID MCNAIRY

DR. VAUGHAN DABBS
This Is Why Your Back HURTS

late to my own funeral
Andrew "Ace" Earp

DEPTH finder

Liza the Ladybug— A Great, Big World

WINGS

The Busy Mom's 10 Minute Guide to a Healthy Happy Family

Anna's Journey
ANNA RENAULY

TRACES
An Autistic Pathway to Creative Expression
Steven Macalester

THE ADVENTURES of FRANKIE FITNESS
Jason Williams

BIG MISTAKE

Louie the Lightning Bug

THE WORD OF THE DAY
31-DAY DEVOTIONAL
TRANSFORMING

MY DAD IS MY HERO

The InHer Me
TERESA E. MACK

MOMMY, LISTEN!

The Perfect Officiant
REVEREND SANDRA BEARDEN

Making Friends around the WORLD

Your Book Here

www.PerfectPublishing.me

www.ingramcontent.com/pod-product-compliance
Lightning Source LLC
Chambersburg PA
CBHW060609200326
41521CB00007B/718